Seeking His Mind

VOICES FROM THE MONASTERY

Seeking His Mind

40 Meetings with Christ

M. Basil Pennington, OCSO

PARACLETE PRESS
BREWSTER, MASSACHUSETTS

2018 Fifth Paperback Printing
2014 Fourth Paperback Printing
2011 Third Paperback Printing
2009 Second Paperback Printing
2007 First Paperback Printing
2002 First Hardcover Printing

Seeking His Mind

ISBN 978-1-55725-562-4

The Library of Congress has catalogued the hardcover edition as follows:
Library of Congress Cataloging-in-Publication Data
Pennington, M. Basil.
   Seeking His mind : 40 meetings with Christ / M. Basil Pennington.
      p. cm.
   ISBN 1-55725-308-0
   1 Jesus Christ—Meditations.   I. Title.
BT306.43.P46   2002
242—dc21   2002008366

10 9 8 7 6 5

Published by Paraclete Press
Brewster, Massachusetts
www.paracletepress.com

Printed in the United States of America

Let the same mind be in you that was in Christ Jesus,
who, though he was in the form of God,
did not regard equality with God
as something to be exploited,
but emptied himself,
taking the form of a slave,
being born in human likeness.
And being found in human form,
he humbled himself
and became obedient to the point of death—
even death on a cross.

PHILIPPIANS 2:5–8

Now we have received not the spirit of the world, but
the Spirit that is from God, so that we may understand
the gifts bestowed on us by God. And we speak of these
things in words not taught by human wisdom but taught
by the Spirit, interpreting spiritual things to those who are
spiritual. . . .

"For who has known the mind of the Lord
so as to instruct him?"
But we have the mind of Christ.

I CORINTHIANS 2:12–13, 16

Contents

Passion and Resurrection

Preface

Anyone who has been in love or who has had a close friendship will understand. I look forward every day to meeting the Lord in lectio. It is a time of intimacy, of heart to heart. We know the Lord is truly present in his inspired Word. Here I find him and eagerly wait to hear what he has to say to me. "Speak, Lord, your servant, your friend, your disciple, wants to hear." I never know what he is going to say. And oftentimes he does quite surprise me. His gift is always a word of life, whether it is an immediate flash of light or a word I must carry with me for a time before it shines forth. This is the excitement of lectio. (In the next chapter I will unpack more fully what this word "lectio" means in our ongoing Christian tradition.) It is a meeting that overflows and energizes the whole of the day, the whole of my life. Through his word, which I carry with me from my daily lectio, I see things differently, in a new, insightful way, according to the mind of Christ.

I am grateful that I have had the joy and privilege through the years of sharing with my fellow travelers some of the words the Lord has spoken to me in the course of my daily lectio. These brief sharings have appeared in the newspapers from Hong Kong to Brooklyn. The Internet has carried them into the homes and hearts of hundreds of friends. And the feedback has indicated that the Lord has spoken them there also, creating bonds among us that have multiplied our joy in the word.

LaVonne Neff and the folks at Paraclete have done a good job, not only in gathering up these sharings, but also of giving them an illuminating setting by placing them in the chronology of our Lord's life. He is the Way. We walk along with him, and we learn the Truth that gives us Life and leads us to the fullness of life. As you share these words now, may you find in them a joy, a fuller life, the blossoming of a friendship.

†M. Basil Pennington, OCSO

Lectio:
A Christian Way to Transformation

A shrinking global village with its increasingly mobile population often gifts us with very interesting and enriching neighbors. This has been our experience at St. Joseph's Abbey. Among our neighbors are a Hindu ashram and a Buddhist meditation center. Swami Satchidananda established to the south a large, prosperous monastery which his disciples refer to as Yogaville East. To the north there is an Insight Meditation Center of the Theravada tradition. I am happy to say that relations with these brothers and sisters are the very best. We mutually share by invitation in each other's special festive celebrations. The Buddhist center especially has encouraged Christians who come there to learn meditation to visit the abbey to get help to integrate their new practice into the context of their Christian life and practice.

Periodically there are persons who make the rounds. They go to the ashram and learn what they can of the eight limbs of Yoga. They spend some time at the meditation center learning insight meditation. And then they knock at the monastery door and ask, "What is your method?"

My usual answer is that our whole life is our method. As the early Christians expressed it, we have entered into "The Way." Our Master and Lord, who spoke of himself as "the Way and the Truth and the Life," coming from the fullness of the Jewish tradition, summed up his way in the two great commandments: "The first and greatest commandment is this: You shall love the Lord your God with your whole mind, your whole heart, your whole soul, and your whole strength. And the second is like unto this: You shall love your neighbor as yourself." He went on to modify the second, saying: "I give you a new commandment: You shall love one another as I have loved you." Making it clear that "greater love than this no one hath than one lay down one's life for one's friend," he went on to do just that: He laid down his life for all of us, his friends.

This is the way of the Christian: that we love the Lord our God and one another, even to the point of laying down our lives for each other. Actual physical martyrdom may be the exception, though it is more common today than in any previous period of Christian history. But we are all called to take up our cross daily and follow our Master. "Unless the grain of wheat fall into the ground and die, it remains itself alone. But if it dies, it will bear much fruit."

This response, that our whole life is our method, usually does not satisfy insistent inquirers. They have found among the Hindus and Buddhists a seemingly rather concise method or practice, and they are looking for the same among the Christians. At this point, insisting always that the practice must nurture a full pursuit of "The Way," and that outside of such a context it may well be fruitless in the deepest sense of that word—we are to judge a tree by its fruit—I tell our inquirers that our method is *lectio*.

"What is that?" is the usual response to such a statement.

I deliberately leave the word in Latin, for the simple translation "reading" certainly betrays the meaning.

More important, *lectio*, or *lectio divina*, always connotes for the Christian coming out of our tradition a whole process summed up in the four words *lectio*, *meditatio*, *oratio*, and *contemplatio*. This process is geared towards a transformation of consciousness and life. "Let this mind be in you which was in Christ Jesus," says St. Paul. Our aim is to have the "mind of Christ," the *nous Christou*, to see things, to evaluate all things, to respond to reality in the way Christ our Lord and Master does—to see things as God sees them, to share in the divine consciousness. Let me develop now this Christian way or process.

Lectio cannot simply mean "reading," even though that is its literal translation. We are speaking of a way of Christian spirituality that prevailed through many centuries when the vast number of Christian people could not read. I think *lectio* here can most properly be understood as meaning "to receive the revelation." It can be perceived immediately that this is a way most consonant with Christianity. We Christians, sharing this in part with our Jewish brothers and sisters, are sons and daughters of the Book. God, who of old spoke first through the creation and then through the prophets, has in these last days spoken to us through his incarnate Son, our Lord Jesus.

Lectio most properly resides in hearing the word of God. We do this as a Christian people when we gather in our communal worship. The Reformers of the sixteenth century quite rightly laid great emphasis on this. The recent liturgical reforms in the Roman Catholic church have also emphasized this.

In an earlier period, memories seem to have been sharper, or were used more. It was not uncommon for an average Christian to know by heart extensive passages of Scripture, perhaps even the whole of the Gospels and the

Psalter. Men like the venerable Abbot Bernard of Clairvaux were reputed to know the whole Bible. These Christians, then, always carried the Scriptures with them and at any moment, drawing on memory, could hear the word of God.

The word of God revealed itself in other ways, too: in the shared faith of sisters and brothers. The Reformers laid great stress on the sermon, as did the Fathers, whose great sermons have come down to us. Faith is also shared in less formal settings, in small groups, or in the one-to-one encounter. Out of our experience of the word, enlightened by the Holy Spirit, we speak the word to one another.

The word can be heard through other media. Music, certainly. Powerful hymns repeat themselves insistently within us: "Amazing grace, how sweet the sound." Art, the frescoes, icons, and stained glass windows. The earliest Christian assemblies, gathering in homes and catacombs, adorned the walls of their meeting places with scenes from the Scriptures. Our eastern Christian sisters and brothers find a real presence in the icons and enshrine them in their homes as well as in their churches. The whole of the Scriptures is depicted in the windows of the great medieval cathedrals, such as Chartres.

The Master Artist does not cease to reveal himself in his masterpiece, the creation. As St. Paul reminded the Romans, for the mind that would see, God has always been there to be seen. Bernard of Clairvaux is noted for the saying that has been rendered into rather trite English: "I have found God more in the trees and the brooks than in the books." Above all does God reveal himself in that which is greatest in all creation, his own image and likeness, the graced person. In others, and in our very selves, we can experience the goodness and love of God, God himself, if we would but be still and know that he is God.

In colloquial English we have the expression: "I read you." It implies that I fully get what someone is trying to convey to me. This is perhaps a good translation of *lectio*, to "read" in this sense: to get God and all he is saying in all the many ways he is speaking.

An Ancient Method

Lectio, then, does not necessarily mean sitting with a book. It can mean looking at a work of art, standing before an icon, listening to a friend's word of faith, or taking a walk, letting the beauty of the creation, that often lies beneath layers of sin's ugliness, speak to us. But for most of us, the most constant, chosen, and privileged hearing of the word will be when we sit daily with the Book, the inspired Word of God. I would like at this point to take a few minutes to share a very simple and practical way of doing our daily *lectio*. This simple method comes from the age-old practice of the monks and nuns as expressed in their customaries. I will present it in three points, for that seems a very traditional way to do it and aids memory.

1. *Come into Presence and call upon the Spirit.* The old monastic usages say that when a nun or monk is going to do *lectio*, she or he takes the Holy Scriptures, kneels, prays to Holy Spirit, reads the first sentence, and then reverently kisses the sacred text. We have two elements here: coming into the presence of God dwelling in his inspired word, and asking his Holy Spirit to help us in our *lectio*.

If one enters the abbatial church at St. Joseph's Abbey (and this is not the only place one will find this), one will always find two lamps burning: one burns before the tabernacle, proclaiming the real presence of Christ in the Eucharist; the other burns before the sacred text enthroned in the middle of the choir, proclaiming a real presence of Christ the Word in his Scriptures. The Word abides in the Bible ever ready to speak to us. Our Bibles should never be just put on the shelf with other books or left lying haphazardly on our desks. They should be enshrined in our homes and offices, proclaiming a real presence. When we come to our *lectio*, we take the book with great reverence and respond to that presence. The monastic customary had the monk kneel before his Lord and, after listening to his first words, kiss the text as a sign of reverence and homage. It is good to bring even our bodies into our acknowledgement of this presence; we are incarnate persons. Acknowledging the Lord's presence in his word, we are ready to listen.

And we call upon Holy Spirit to help us to hear. In his last discourse at the supper on the night before he died, Jesus promised to send Holy Spirit, the Paraclete, to abide with us, to teach us, and to call to mind all he had taught us. It is Holy Spirit who inspired the writers of the Sacred Text. This same Holy Spirit dwells in us. We ask him now to make the message, the word of life in the text he inspired, come alive now for us and truly speak to us.

2. *We listen for ten or fifteen minutes.* I say ten or fifteen minutes. One can choose any length of time that satisfies, but ten or fifteen minutes can be enough for the Lord to give us a word of life. We are busy people; it is difficult for us to make time—we don't find it, we have to make it—for all the things we want to do each day. But who cannot make ten minutes for something if he or she really wants to? The point here is that we listen for

a period of time. The nun or monk will usually sit at her or his *lectio* until the next bell rings. You do not usually have bells to summon you from one thing to another, but you can set a time. What we want to avoid is setting a goal for ourselves to read a page, a chapter, or a section. We are so programmed to speed reading, to getting things done, that if we set ourselves to read a certain amount, we will be pushed to get it done. We do not want that. We want to be able to listen to the Word freely. If he speaks to us in the first or second sentence, we want to be free to abide there and let that word of life resound in us, going on only when we feel we have responded to him as fully as we wish for the moment. If in our *lectio* time we hear only a sentence or two—fine! The important thing is to hear the Word, to let him speak to us. That is why in the second point we say "we listen," not "we read."

3. *At the end of our time, we take a word and thank the Lord.* "We thank the Lord"—it is a wonderful thing that at any time we wish we can get God almighty, our Lord God, to sit down and speak to us. We often have to make appointments and do a lot of waiting to get his representatives to give us some time and attention. But not so with the Lord. This moment of thanksgiving emphasizes again the real presence. God has truly made himself available to us and spoken to us through his word; we thank him.

"We take a word." *Word* here does not mean necessarily a single word; it can connote a sentence or a phrase. It means a meaningful message summed up in one or a few words. In the earliest Christian times, devout women and men would go to a spiritual mother or father and ask them for a "word of life," a brief directive that would guide them in the way of Christian holiness.

A man asked Amma Syncletica, "Give me a word." The old woman said, "If you observe the following you can be saved: Be joyful at all times, pray without ceasing, and give thanks in all things."

Abba Pambo asked Abba Anthony, "What ought I to do?" and the old man said to him, "Do not trust in your own righteousness, do not worry about the past, control your tongue and your stomach."

Brother Bruno asked Father Basil, "Give me a word of life, Father." "Say, 'I am God's son,' and live accordingly," was the reply.

As we listen to the Lord in our daily *lectio*, we ask him for a word of life. Some days he does very clearly speak to us. Some word or phrase of the text seems virtually to shout at us. He speaks and we hear him. Many of us have had our Taboric or Damascus moments. Such words change our lives and remain always with us, never far from our consciousness. Other times his word is not so dramatically spoken. And there are days when he does not seem to speak at all. We read on and on, listening, but nothing strikes home. On such days we have to take a word and carry it with us. Often, later in the day, it will speak, if not for us, for another.

Guerric of Igny, a twelfth-century Cistercian monk, in an Easter sermon comments on the gospel scene where the three women who failed to find Christ at the empty tomb suddenly encounter him on the garden path. Guerric says to his brothers: "You know how it is, brothers. Some days we go to our *lectio* and the Lord is not there; we go to the tomb of the altar and he is not there; and then, as we are going out to work, lo, halfway down the garden path we meet him." The word we have taken may suddenly come alive for us as we are conversing with someone else, or drying the dishes, or puzzling over something altogether different.

From *Lectio* to *Contemplatio*

If each day a word of the Lord can truly come alive for us and can form our mind and heart, we will come indeed to live by faith as just persons; we will have that mind of Christ. This is precisely the aim of *meditatio*.

Again, I hesitate to translate the word *meditatio* directly. Meditation has come to have various meanings for us. Perhaps the most prevalent meaning is that given to it in modern English Hindu terminology. This may be a commentary on how poorly we Christians have made our own heritage present and available. We have all heard of transcendental meditation. In this Eastern sense, meditation means a certain emptiness, openness, presence to the absolute, to the no-thingness, the beyond, and the practices that seek to take us into such a state. In more recent Christian usage, meditation has meant searching out the facts and mysteries of revelation to understand them better, to be moved to respond to them, and to bring their influence into our lives. It has been largely a rational exercise ordered toward affective and effective response. *Meditatio* in the earlier Christian tradition has a meaning that perhaps can be seen as lying somewhere between these two modern meanings. *Meditatio* in this tradition meant repeating the word one had received from *lectio*—whatever form it took: reading, the faith sharing of a father, the proclamation in the assembly—repeating it perhaps on the lips, at least in the mind, until it formed the heart; until, as the Fathers sometimes expressed it, the mind descended into the heart. On a couple of occasions, St. Luke in his Gospel tells us that Mary pondered or weighed certain events in her heart. He is pointing toward meditation of this sort. The word is allowed simply to be there, letting its weight, its own gravity, press upon us till it gives form to the attitude of our heart. The result is *oratio*.

Again, I hesitate to translate *oratio* simply as "prayer." Too easily do we think of prayer as asking God for something or conversing with him or saying prayers. All of that is indeed prayer and can be good prayer. But here, when the Fathers speak of *oratio*, they mean something different; they mean something very powerful and urgent: fiery prayer, darts of fire that shoot out from the heart into the very heart of God. As the psalmist sings: "In my meditation fire burst forth." It is prayer in the Holy Spirit. It is brief. It is total. When the word finally penetrates and touches the core of our being, it calls forth this powerful response, whether it be a cry of praise, love, petition, thanksgiving, reparation, or some mixture of all of these, according to the particular word and circumstances. This is pure prayer. For a moment it takes us beyond ourselves. It calls forth from us a response so complete that for the moment we are wholly in the response. For a moment we leave behind all consideration of ourselves, all the usual self-reflection or self-awareness; we are totally in the response. It is a moment when we fulfill the first and greatest commandment: We love the Lord our God with our whole mind, our whole heart, our whole soul, and all our strength.

Such moments are very special, very wonderful. We want them to return, we want them to go on and on; in a word, we want *contemplatio*. For this is what contemplation means in this tradition: the word has so formed us and called us forth, that we abide in total response. Our whole being is a yes to God as he has revealed himself to us. We are, as the Book of Revelation says of Christ, an Amen to the Father.

This transformation of consciousness we cannot bring about by ourselves. It is beyond us. We can prepare ourselves for it, seek it, and dispose ourselves for it. We can actively prepare for it by seeking to let go of the things that have a hold on us and keep us from being free to be a complete yes to God. This is the role of self-denial or mortification. Our Master spoke of taking up our cross daily, denying ourselves, dying to self: "Unless the grain of wheat fall in the ground and die . . . " We have to be willing to let go of self, that constant watching of self, that wanting to be right, to be always correct; and turn both eyes, our whole attention, on God, so that we can truly and freely hear his word. We seek this transformation by listening to the word of God with openness, letting it in and letting it reform us, through *lectio* and *meditatio*. We can dispose ourselves for transformation by making spaces for God to come in and reveal himself in himself, and in that revealing, transform us. "Be still," he says, "and know that I am God."

Waiting on the Lord

God made us. He knows us through and through, and he respects us as no one else does. He knows the greatest thing he has given us is our freedom, because therein lies our power to love, to be like him who is love. He respects our freedom. He will never force his way into our lives: "Behold, I stand at the door and knock. And if one opens, I will come in . . . " We first open the door by *lectio*; we further open it by silent attentive presence. When the received word has formed our hearts and, through the passing experiences of fiery prayer, creates in us a desire for an abiding transformation, an abiding state of prayer in presence, we begin to want to cultivate interior quietness, silence, and space in expectant longing. The Fathers have passed down to us a method for cultivating this prayer of the heart. Centering prayer is a modern presentation of this traditional method. But any method is only dispositive. It is a concrete way of asking, of seeking. Contemplative prayer remains a gift. We dispose ourselves in a stillness that expresses an intent, loving longing. And then he comes, when he wills. Much of our time may be spent in expectant, silent waiting. We may murmur again and again his name, our word of love and longing. But we can only wait till he comes and with his touch draws us forth beyond ourselves into the knowledge, the experiential knowledge, of himself, which transforms our consciousness. According as he gives, this transformed state of consciousness becomes more abiding, until by his grace and mercy it quietly prevails even in the midst of our many activities. In this state of consciousness we come to see things as he sees them, value them as he values them. We seek to become full collaborators with him in bringing about by love and service the redeeming transformation of the world. I will not develop here at length the effects of this lived transformation of consciousness, but I think one can readily surmise how it will affect our relationships with others, and with the rest of creation. It certainly provides the base for global community and ecological reverence.

Most striking about this Christian way to transformation is its simplicity. We have but to open ourselves to the revealing and all-powerful word of God and he will do the rest. It is simple, but not easy. For such openness implies making time and space to hear. Making time is difficult enough in our busy lives. Making space in our cluttered hearts is more difficult, for if each day we take the next step in faithfulness to his revealing word, in the end we will have to give up everything. But this is only in order to have the space to find everything, with him and in him, in all its potential fullness and magnificence, no longer bound by the confines of our limitations. In this way we come to live the first great commandment to love the Lord our God with our whole mind, our whole heart, our whole soul, and our whole strength; and the second, which is like unto it, to love our neighbors and the whole creation as we love ourselves in that first great love. It is to be wholly in "The Way," who is the way to the Father in the Holy Spirit of Love.

Beginnings

1 | *Imagining Scripture*

1 CORINTHIANS 2:6–16

*Yet among the mature we do speak wisdom, though
it is not a wisdom of this age or of the rulers of this
age, who are doomed to perish. But we speak God's
wisdom, secret and hidden, which God decreed before
the ages for our glory. None of the rulers of this age
understood this; for if they had, they would not have
crucified the Lord of glory. But, as it is written,*
> *"What no eye has seen, nor ear heard,*
> *nor the human heart conceived,*
> *what God has prepared for those who love*
> *him"—*

*these things God has revealed to us through the Spirit;
for the Spirit searches everything, even the depths
of God. For what human being knows what is truly
human except the human spirit that is within? So also
no one comprehends what is truly God's except the
Spirit of God. Now we have received not the spirit
of the world, but the Spirit that is from God, so that
we may understand the gifts bestowed on us by God.
And we speak of these things in words not taught by
human wisdom but taught by the Spirit, interpreting
spiritual things to those who are spiritual.*

*Those who are unspiritual do not receive the gifts
of God's Spirit, for they are foolishness to them, and
they are unable to understand them because they are
spiritually discerned. Those who are spiritual discern
all things, and they are themselves subject to no one
else's scrutiny.*

*"For who has known the mind of the Lord
so as to instruct him?"*
But we have the mind of Christ.

I am a teacher of centering prayer, a prayer that goes beyond thoughts and images to God dwelling in the center of our being. We encourage folks to spend an hour a day in prayer, little enough for God who gives us the twenty-four hours.

How do we spend the hour? First, we "center" twice a day for twenty minutes at a time. Centering prayer is based on faith—by faith we know that God dwells within us, with all God's creative love, and wants our love. And faith comes through hearing. So we also spend some time each day in *lectio,* listening to the Lord in his inspired word, especially in the holy Gospels.

It is here—as we listen to the Lord in Scripture—that our imagination comes into play. Some get the idea that because we encourage centering prayer, which goes beyond images, we must be against the use of the imagination. By no means. There is a time and place to use this wonderful faculty God has given us.

If we may speak so anthropomorphically, just think of the imagination God has exercised in creating this wonderful world of ours. How he must have delighted in making all the different flowers and trees with their varied colors, especially in the fall, not to speak of the ever-changing clouds. Think of the animal kingdom, the tropical fish beyond counting, and you and me and all our sisters and brothers—what variety, what imagination!

Perhaps God's most imaginative act was when he decided himself to become a Jewish carpenter, born of a virgin, and to die on a cross to give an ultimate sign of love. And what imagination we see in Jesus. Think of his many stories and parables: the workers in the vineyard, the prodigal son, the good shepherd, the searching housewife, and so many more. Everyday things became fabric for his canvas—"Which of you when your child asks for an egg would give the child a stone?" And there are his many "signs." Did not his imagination reach a summit when he undertook to change bread into his very self and give us to eat? What a sign of self-giving and nurturing love!

His church, the one he founded, continued to use imagination in surrounding this eucharistic sign with a rich, symbolic liturgy taking many forms, ever adapting itself to different peoples and changing times. Imagination is behind the whole sacramental system and the never-ending challenge to find the language (a collection of creative symbols) to express the inexpressible.

The Scriptures resort to imaginative stories and myths to express what is too big for our logical concepts. Letting the Scriptures come alive in our imagination, we have the challenge to hear what they are saying to us today and to share that with others.

Yes, it is not only for the church as a whole, the church as the divinely constituted teacher, but for each one of us to use our imagination to enter into what is beyond and to share what we receive.

My nephew claims to have watched *The Lion King* twenty-three times with his little daughter. Little ones never tire of images and flights of imagination. Jesus said, "Unless you become as little ones, you will not enter the kingdom of heaven." We need to let the Scriptures fill our imaginations and give us the images that will stir our emotions and motivate our wills to seek wholeheartedly what is beyond, but what alone can satisfy our hearts, which are made for the divine.

With *lectio* we are prepared truly to seek God at the center, beyond all the thoughts and images, which are too small for God but which point the way and urge us on. There is a time to imagine. And there is a time to leave images behind.

2 | *Awesome and Humble*

LORD, you were favorable to your land;
you restored the fortunes of Jacob.
You forgave the iniquity of your people;
you pardoned all their sin. Selah
You withdrew all your wrath;
you turned from your hot anger.

Restore us again, O God of our salvation,
and put away your indignation toward us.
Will you be angry with us forever?
Will you prolong your anger to all generations?
Will you not revive us again,
so that your people may rejoice in you?
Show us your steadfast love, O LORD,
and grant us your salvation.

Let me hear what God the LORD will speak,
for he will speak peace to his people,
to his faithful, to those who turn to him in their hearts.
Surely his salvation is at hand for those who fear him,
that his glory may dwell in our land.

Steadfast love and faithfulness will meet;
righteousness and peace will kiss each other.
Faithfulness will spring up from the ground,
and righteousness will look down from the sky.
The LORD will give what is good,
and our land will yield its increase.

Righteousness will go before him,
and will make a path for his steps.

We have been baptized into Christ. Our true life is our life in Christ. We live this life in liturgical mystery as the church year unfolds.

In early December, during the first days of Advent, we live in the expectation that comes from the promise of our God that we sinners do have a Savior. In the days that follow, we celebrate the coming of our Savior, a celebration that reaches its completion in the Feast of the Presentation on February 2. Mary, in fulfillment of the law of promise, brings her Son, the Son of God, into the midst of his chosen people. The scene tells us graphically of the role of the holy Virgin in the economy of salvation. It is through her that all comes to us. And the gift is met with Simeon's troubling prophecy: Mary's Son is set for the rise and fall of many.

As the green days following the Presentation begin to unfold, we experience our Savior's humanity. As he brings his good news to the multitudes, he is in danger of being mobbed. He seeks help. He uses Peter's small fragile bark as a pulpit—a symbolic act indeed. And Peter's humble service is amply rewarded: fish in abundance. Peter must shout for the help of others. Again, a most significant act: Peter needs the help of others to care for the Lord's catch.

This One who can herd fish by the hundreds into a net, he is the awesome One who set Isaiah trembling, in need of a fiery coal to purify his lips before he could speak of him (Isaiah 6:1–7). He is the awesome One, and now he needs a poor little boat to serve him. He created all and gave all, and he rewards the simple use of one of his gifts.

It is difficult to put it all together. Awesome God— humble preacher. We tend to fall on one side or the other. We keep him at a distance, in his heavens. We adore him, worship him, tremble before him, and for the most part try to forget him, because it is no fun to live trembling. Or we bring him down to our size: a good man, understanding, ready to help, not too demanding. Certainly not to be feared.

It is not either/or. It is both/and.

What do we do with this?

St. Bernard of Clairvaux, one of the first Cistercians, gave some good advice flowing out of his own experience. Commenting on the Song of Songs, he developed the idea of our responding to the divine love with a kiss. He went on to speak of a kiss of the feet, of the hands, and finally of the lips. Moving on with his imagery, he says that the Lord has two feet: one of justice, the other of mercy. And then he speaks of his experience: If I cling too long to the foot of justice, I become full of fear and am close to despair. I must quickly move to the foot of mercy. But if I cling too long to the foot of mercy, I soon become very lax and remiss and in danger of losing my Lord. So I sing both of his mercy and of his justice.

Yes, Christ is the awesome God of Sinai, of Isaiah's visions, of the Book of Revelation. He is to be adored, and feared, and worshiped, and gratefully loved as the source of all that we are and have. And Christ is equally the gentle, loving carpenter from the hill town of Nazareth, who went about spreading good news, healing and comforting and forgiving all who turned to him. Undoubtedly, someday—maybe only in the vision to come—this will all come together for us. For now, if we would not fall on one side or the other, we, like Bernard, need to watch ourselves, keep our balance, and sing of both the mercy and the justice of the Lord, of both the awesome God and the humble Son, who comes to us in love.

3 | *Mary Brings Jesus*

LUKE 1:39–45

In those days Mary set out and went with haste to a Judean town in the hill country, where she entered the house of Zechariah and greeted Elizabeth. When Elizabeth heard Mary's greeting, the child leaped in her womb. And Elizabeth was filled with the Holy Spirit and exclaimed with a loud cry, "Blessed are you among women, and blessed is the fruit of your womb. And why has this happened to me, that the mother of my Lord comes to me? For as soon as I heard the sound of your greeting, the child in my womb leaped for joy. And blessed is she who believed that there would be a fulfillment of what was spoken to her by the Lord."

For me one of the inspiring, courageous stories of the Bible is the story of the event that we call the Visitation. A beautiful young woman who has just become pregnant, who has just been told she is the mother of God, forgetting herself, heads off across an alien land to bring succor to an aged cousin.

I daresay most women, on becoming pregnant, especially with their first pregnancy, begin to center a bit more on self. Should the mother of God be running off to serve the mother of her son's forerunner? Should it not be just the opposite? At least, should she not be allowed to rest at home in safety, surrounded by loving care? And how was Joseph going to handle this? Shouldn't she stay and work this out with him before her condition becomes obvious? And what of the dangers of the journey? The hostility of the Samaritans was proverbial, and she would be traveling alone.

The angel didn't tell Mary she should go. The divine messenger only announced her cousin's condition. Mary was certainly in a unique position to accompany her elderly cousin in her extraordinary pregnancy, and no doubt a part of Mary longed to have a female friend with whom she could share her own growing experience. But her compassionate heart was for her cousin. So off she went.

Only on seven occasions do the Gospels recount a word from the mouth of the mother of God. But on this occasion we are not even told what the words were. Perhaps it is to leave the space open, for when Mary comes to us her presence is expressed in so many different ways. In any case, cousin Elizabeth clues us in: "As soon as I heard the sound of your greeting . . ." The simple experience of Mary's presence was all that mattered.

Then what? The child in Elizabeth's womb leaped for joy, being filled with Holy Spirit. Elizabeth herself was filled with a discerning spirit, calling Mary "the mother of my Lord"—she recognized her at once.

I believe this particular incident is recounted in the opening pages of the Gospel, as our Savior begins his salvific mission, to invite us to be aware of Mary's oft-hidden but very important role in the story of salvation.

It is she who brings Christ, to sanctify, to fill with leaping joy, to enlighten, to console and comfort and strengthen. This is Mary's mission in history and in the life of each one of us.

It is Mary who brings Christ to us. And she brings us a faith that can withstand even the test of a Holy Saturday, when the faith of all others seems to fail. When we sense her presence, we gain courage, comfort, hope, and joy and direction.

We do not know how Elizabeth, who had concealed herself during this time of wondrous pregnancy, and Mary spent the next three months. But we can well imagine the sharing that went on. It was all new for Elizabeth, though she was a few months ahead of her young cousin in the maternal experience. But Mary was the one of blessed faith, a faith Elizabeth's elderly husband had failed to bring her, and Mary's faith helped to make sense of Elizabeth's mysterious pregnancy.

If we give Mary a chance, not only will she bring Christ ever more fully into our lives with the joy of salvation, she will abide with us. She will be our life, our sweetness, and our hope. Mary will be with us as we face the vicissitudes and mysteries of life. If we have the ears to hear them, the words of the dying Christ still ring in our ears: "Behold your mother." Mary will come into our lives with her divine Son to the extent that we are open and ready to welcome them.

4 | *John the Baptizer, Witness and Friend*

LUKE 1:57–66

*Now the time came for Elizabeth to give birth, and
she bore a son. Her neighbors and relatives heard
that the Lord had shown his great mercy to her, and
they rejoiced with her.*

*On the eighth day they came to circumcise the
child, and they were going to name him Zechariah
after his father. But his mother said, "No; he is to
be called John." They said to her, "None of your
relatives has this name." Then they began motion-
ing to his father to find out what name he wanted to
give him. He asked for a writing tablet and wrote,
"His name is John." And all of them were amazed.
Immediately his mouth was opened and his tongue
freed, and he began to speak, praising God. Fear
came over all their neighbors, and all these things
were talked about throughout the entire hill country
of Judea. All who heard them pondered them and said,
"What then will this child become?" For, indeed, the
hand of the Lord was with him.*

It was the talk of Jerusalem and all the region.
After all, the child's father had been struck
dumb right in the temple. His mother was well
on in years. Then suddenly his father could speak
again. And they gave the child a curious name, at
least curious for that priestly family. The people

who heard about John's birth didn't need to hear about Mary's visit, they didn't need to know that this was the long-awaited prophetic moment, to know that something mysterious was happening. What was going on? Who was this child—another Samuel or Samson? What did the future hold for him? And for them?

Even today, John's birth is uniquely celebrated (his birthday is celebrated on June 24). Along with his cousin and Savior, and the Savior's mother, his is the only birth so celebrated throughout the Christian world.

Monks and nuns have always looked to John as a special patron and model. Like him, they go apart, seeking solitude for prayer and communion with God. His ascetical ideals inspire them, and can indeed inspire all Christians. It was a rigorous asceticism—I don't know what modern nutritionists would say about a diet of honey and wild locusts. Maybe it contains all the necessary nutrients. It did turn out a man of exceptional vigor. In any case, John can call all of us to a simpler life.

But of greater significance to us is that he was "a burning and shining lamp" (John 5:35). All his austerity was in service of a mission: to be a clear witness to Christ, a person who would show others how to prepare for Christ, how to find Christ. Even to the first apostles, it was he who pointed the way. John gives witness to us, and he shows us that witness should be an important part of our lives as Christians.

One reason why monks and nuns go apart is to be clear signs, clear witnesses to Christ and his teaching, a prophetic witness that there is a God and that God is worthy of our all. Likewise, every Christian, as he or she walks through this world, wants to be a clear sign pointing to Christ, witnessing to what he taught, this not so much by words, though they have their place, but more by the way the Christian lives, speaks, and responds to others.

When Jesus spoke of John, he pointed to something more significant than the prophetic witness. He spoke of John as his friend—the friend of the Bridegroom. John's whole life was centered on Christ. He shared profoundly in Christ's life and mission from the very beginning, even in the womb. Like a good "best man," his concern was to do all he could to facilitate things for the Bridegroom. With selfless love he proclaimed: "He must increase, but I must decrease" (John 3:30). The selfishness and self-centeredness in our lives must indeed decrease, so that Christ can fill our lives more and more, so that the Christ within us may shine forth more clearly and powerfully. But more, there is to be between each one of us and the Lord a tender, deep, rich intimacy—a true friendship.

The Cistercians have always called their monasteries "schools of love." For this, above all, they go apart: to learn how to be true friends with the Lord, to grow into that friendship, to decrease so he can increase; not only by spending time in prayer, Scripture, and contemplation, but in a total gift of themselves to the community in loving service. Every Christian community should be a school of love, where each comes to know and love Jesus as Friend, and to love and serve him in each other, in the least of his sisters and brothers.

May John, the man from the desert, the ascetic, the burning and shining lamp, help us all to be true friends.

5 | *Tension in the Holy Family*

LUKE 2:40–52

The child grew and became strong, filled with wisdom; and the favor of God was upon him.

Now every year his parents went to Jerusalem for the festival of the Passover. And when he was twelve years old, they went up as usual for the festival. When the festival was ended and they started to return, the boy Jesus stayed behind in Jerusalem, but his parents did not know it. Assuming that he was in the group of travelers, they went a day's journey. Then they started to look for him among their relatives and friends. When they did not find him, they returned to Jerusalem to search for him. After three days they found him in the temple, sitting among the teachers, listening to them and asking them questions. And all who heard him were amazed at his understanding and his answers. When his parents saw him they were astonished; and his mother said to him, "Child, why have you treated us like this? Look, your father and I have been searching for you in great anxiety." He said to them, "Why were you searching for me? Did you not know that I must be in my Father's house?" But they did not understand what he said to them. Then he went down with them and came to Nazareth, and was obedient to them. His mother treasured all these things in her heart.

And Jesus increased in wisdom and in years, and in divine and human favor.

On the Feast of the Holy Family (the Sunday after Christmas) we hear the Gospel account of the loss and finding of Jesus at the time of his family's pilgrimage to Jerusalem, when he was twelve, a story that has many touching aspects

What family could be holier than this family? And yet here Jesus causes worry, tension, and anxiety, and Mary gives vent to her anger—with all the pathos of a good Jewish mother.

By God's mercy and grace, our monastic community is a holy family, and we come from holy families. Yet some of us monks have painfully had to live through the experience of causing disappointment and anger in our families, when we left them and joined our monastic family. Many of those whom we loved saw our joining this family as something like a bad marriage—at least until they got to know this wonderful family we had joined.

Within the daily life of our monastic family, as in any family, some cause tension and others give vent to their anger. Looking to the Holy Family, we need to remember that this can be done without any fault or sin. Certainly Jesus was sinless. It may seem to us that he could have warned Mary and Joseph. He didn't. Why? Perhaps circumstances were such that this was not possible. The occasion and inspiration to be about his Father's business arose, and he could not get to them in time.

Even if we grant that, I must confess that if I were the father of that twelve-year-old and he answered his mother's expression of anguish the way Jesus did, I would have been sorely tempted to let him experience a bit of my anger. The fact is, we often do not really understand what is going on in the other. What seems to us as dead wrong, they, according to their lights, see as the right thing to do. And they find it hard to understand why everyone else doesn't see it that way too.

We cannot control all the emotions that rise in us. What we can do is this. As persons guided by our reason, enlightened by faith and by Holy Spirit through the gifts of the Spirit, we can decide what we will do with our emotions. Mary on this occasion, and perhaps on many other occasions with her teenager, decided to express her anger, or at least her distress. "Child, why have you treated us like this?" (I can easily hear my own mother's voice here.)

If for a while there was tension, incomprehension, and even anger, in the end full harmony and due order were restored. The family returned home, and Jesus was subject to his parents. This was the climate for growth. And Jesus grew in wisdom, age, and grace. Here is the important point of this teaching (and the gospel stories are meant not so much to relate historical events as to teach): It is human to have misunderstandings, to cause tension and pain, to feel deeply about things. But whatever the misunderstanding, pain, or grievance, whatever the feelings and emotions, we need to let them go, and go on being a family of caring love.

If this Holy Family could experience such tension and anger, then indeed we should not be surprised to find a certain amount of the same in our own holy families. If we can accept that even the holiest and sinless do cause tension, and do express their frustration and anger—accept it and pass beyond it and go on in a climate of love and care—we will have families in which we all grow in wisdom, age, and grace.

6 | *Good Work*

1 THESSALONIANS 4:9–12

*Now concerning love of the brothers and sisters,
you do not need to have anyone write to you, for
you yourselves have been taught by God to love one
another; and indeed you do love all the brothers
and sisters throughout Macedonia. But we urge you,
beloved, to do so more and more, to aspire to live
quietly, to mind your own affairs, and to work with
your hands, as we directed you, so that you may
behave properly toward outsiders and be dependent
on no one.*

St. Benedict certainly held labor in high regard:
"When they live by the labor of their hands, like
our Fathers and the Apostles, then they are truly
monks." He could have chosen a yet even more
sublime model: the Lord Jesus himself. The greater
part of the short time Jesus, God's own Son, spent
on earth was spent as a laborer, planing wood and
fitting it, delivering orders and bringing in supplies.
Later he would choose mostly laborers to form his
chosen band, though "white collar" workers were
not left out. Paul, that apostle-come-lately, though a
well-educated rabbi, prided himself on living by the
labor of his own hands. The Fathers of Egypt, the

first Christian monks, were known to weave and unweave baskets to keep busy; more practically, they also raised grain and sent it down the river to the poor of Alexandria.

There are many aspects to labor: It provides for our own needs; it frees us from idleness; it offers us an opportunity to serve others, either immediately or through giving alms; it is the divinely chosen penance, an opportunity to make reparation for our sins; it is prayer; it is collaborating with God in bringing his creation to its consummation; it is a call to glorify the Maker of All. Undoubtedly, some forms of work seem to reveal one aspect and others, another. Our own attitudes will incline us habitually or occasionally to emphasize one or another of these dimensions. The important thing is not to fall into a shallow or materialistic outlook, where work is just work or has only its own materialistic ends. Such work is not worthy of those who are made in the image of God.

We do have to make a living. Jobs do need to get done. Works of art have their own intrinsic beauty. Ordering our work to higher goals will not detract from all this. It will only enhance these ends, incorporate them into the overall thrust of life, and augment our dedication to accomplishing them, doing the work well to the best of our ability.

We have our work. It will be more meaningful for us, whatever it may be, if we take all the opportunities it affords to serve and give joy to others; if we reverence things we work with and are conscious that our working with them gives them an opportunity to express themselves at a higher level through our activity and love; if we share some of the fruit of our labor with those less fortunate; if we do all for the love and glory of God, knowing then that our work is part of the transformation of the whole of creation, including especially ourselves.

7 | *Calling the Twelve*

MARK 3:13–15

He went up the mountain and called to him those whom he wanted, and they came to him. And he appointed twelve, whom he also named apostles, to be with him, and to be sent out to proclaim the message, and to have authority to cast out demons.

Mark tells us, early in his narration of Jesus' public ministry, that Jesus went up onto a mountain and called those he wanted. God had come into our midst in Christ so that we might find our place in the midst of God. His descent into the creation reached its depths when he stood in the waters of the Jordan with the fish swimming about him. As he rose up out of the waters and was confirmed by the Father's voice and the Spirit's descent upon him, he began the homeward journey to Jerusalem, Calvary, resurrection, and ascension to the Father's right hand.

So here he very symbolically goes up the mountain. He has begun his ascent. And he calls to this height, to this new level of consciousness, those whom he wants. The throng, whom he has come to save and will save, remain on the plain. Many are called, few are chosen. His is the freedom to call. What a grace it is to be called by him.

The call does not usually come in the form of a tap on the shoulder. Rarely does he send an angel as he did to Mary of Nazareth, or even a saint as he did to Joan of Arc. The call more often comes in the form of a moment of insight in the midst of our musings—perhaps as we read an article such as this, or through the sharing of a friend. We have to remain in listening mode, or we may well miss it.

He called those whom he wanted to call, and St. Mark tells us they came to him. The call respects our freedom. The response demands our freedom. It is up to us, when we hear the call, to come in response.

Those who were called, Mark goes on to tell us, were called to be with him and to be sent out. This at first sounds like a paradox. How can they do both?

I think this tells us that, first of all, we are to be with him. It is folly to try to be apostolic, to go out to help others, if we have not first connected with the Lord and become one with him. Conversely, the more we are with him, the more we are one with his life and mission—which is precisely to be sent out by the Father into this world for the salvation of all. So the more we are with him, the more we are sent out, however the apostolic love expresses itself in our particular vocation.

Even the most enclosed contemplatives, if they are one with Jesus, are fired with apostolic love, a love which, in their case, expresses itself through praying that the Lord send laborers into the fields, and through prayerfully supporting those laborers. Others go into the fields as one with Christ, to cast out the demons and bring the good news of salvation, to bring peace and joy in Christ through hope, whether through preaching and teaching or through the powerful witness of daily Christian life. Listen. Hear his call. Come to him. Be with him. And do whatever he tells you.

8 | *We Are All Called*

JOHN 1:43–51

The next day Jesus decided to go to Galilee. He found Philip and said to him, "Follow me." Now Philip was from Bethsaida, the city of Andrew and Peter. Philip found Nathanael and said to him, "We have found him about whom Moses in the law and also the prophets wrote, Jesus son of Joseph from Nazareth." Nathanael said to him, "Can anything good come out of Nazareth?" Philip said to him, "Come and see." When Jesus saw Nathanael coming toward him, he said of him, "Here is truly an Israelite in whom there is no deceit!" Nathanael asked him, "Where did you get to know me?" Jesus answered, "I saw you under the fig tree before Philip called you." Nathanael replied, "Rabbi, you are the Son of God! You are the King of Israel!" Jesus answered, "Do you believe because I told you that I saw you under the fig tree? You will see greater things than these." And he said to him, "Very truly, I tell you, you will see heaven opened and the angels of God ascending and descending upon the Son of Man."

As Christians, followers of Jesus Christ, we are eager to know what the Lord wants of us. How are we, one with him, to live our lives to the fullest for the glory of the Father and the well-being of the whole human family? In a word, we want to know our vocation. For we know that in doing God's will in union with Christ, we can come to the greatest possible fulfillment and joy, and our life can have the greatest possible meaning.

In the Gospels we hear many vocation stories. The Lord calls the twelve chosen to be his apostles; he calls the seventy-two disciples and sends them forth in mission. Some of those he cures are called to follow him; others are sent back to give witness among their own people. The Lord responds to generosity and faith with a call to greater intimacy.

Sometimes his call is heeded without the least bit of hesitation. Sometimes there is questioning, even skepticism leading to hesitation. And, sad to say, sometimes the response to the divine call is a no.

Sometimes the call is accompanied with a sign, as on the day Jesus called the apostle Nathanael (who in the Gospels is also named Bartholomew). With a prophetic word Jesus made it clear to this skeptical young man that he was always under Jesus' caring eye. "I saw you under the fig tree before Philip called you."

Most of us probably won't receive a clear sign like Nathanael's, though there may be coincidences that set us to wondering. I remember a Jewish friend one day asking me: "Do you know what a coincidence is?" Of course I said, "No." And she enlightened me: "A coincidence is God working anonymously." God is at work in our lives in so many more ways than we usually know.

Even if we do not receive a clear sign, we may hear a call, when a friend, like Philip, shares with us an enthusiasm for the Lord and calls us to action: "We have found him about whom Moses in the law and also the prophets wrote, Jesus son of Joseph from Nazareth."

And, like Nathanael, we may first react with skepticism: "Can anything good come out of Nazareth?" The Lord often comes into our lives in amazing and unexpected ways. He is the God of surprises.

Nathanael was thoroughly skeptical, but he listened to the call coming through his friend and responded with a certain openness. He was rewarded with a sign. And no matter how the call first reaches us, in the end we, like Nathanael, will come to know deep within that even before the call—indeed, from all eternity—the Lord saw us and was himself beckoning to us to come and follow him. The peace, the joy, and the meaningfulness we find in a life in which we choose to follow the Lord—these are the signs for us that we have indeed heard the Lord's call and are following him.

Vocations are not only to the priesthood and religious life. Certainly, we as a Christian community very much need priests to lead us in the Eucharist and bring us the sacramental life. We are deeply enriched by the witness and ministry of religious, whether they be active religious or those living hidden in the cloister, who, as a community, give us a powerful witness to the allness of God and the hope that is ours. But married life and singleness in the world are also calls coming from the Master, and they are equally important for building up the Kingdom and giving glory to the Father.

May we each have that openness and attentiveness that enable us to hear the Lord's call, however it might come to us. In the encounter may we, like Nathanael, cry out: "Lord, you are the Son of God." And may we have the grace and courage to follow wherever he may call us.

9 | *Where Are the Men?*

JOHN 15:1–17

*I am the true vine, and my Father is the vinegrower.
He removes every branch in me that bears no fruit.
Every branch that bears fruit he prunes to make it
bear more fruit. You have already been cleansed by
the word that I have spoken to you. Abide in me as
I abide in you. Just as the branch cannot bear fruit
by itself unless it abides in the vine, neither can you
unless you abide in me. I am the vine, you are the
branches. Those who abide in me and I in them
bear much fruit, because apart from me you can do
nothing. Whoever does not abide in me is thrown
away like a branch and withers; such branches are
gathered, thrown into the fire, and burned. If you
abide in me, and my words abide in you, ask for
whatever you wish, and it will be done for you. My
Father is glorified by this, that you bear much fruit
and become my disciples. As the Father has loved me,
so I have loved you; abide in my love. If you keep my
commandments, you will abide in my love, just as I
have kept my Father's commandments and abide in
his love. I have said these things to you so that my joy
may be in you, and that your joy may be complete.*

*This is my commandment, that you love one
another as I have loved you. No one has greater love
than this, to lay down one's life for one's friends.
You are my friends if you do what I command you.
I do not call you servants any longer, because the
servant does not know what the master is doing; but*

I have called you friends, because I have made known to you
everything that I have heard from my Father. You did not
choose me but I chose you. And I appointed you to go and
bear fruit, fruit that will last, so that the Father will give you
whatever you ask him in my name. I am giving you these
commands so that you may love one another.

I was driving to the airport with Tilden Edwards, the founder of Shalem, a wonderful ecumenical center of spirituality in Washington, D.C. I had just come from an exciting gathering of the Contemplative Outreach, celebrating the Year of Jubilee. As we shared our experiences, we both realized that our gatherings brought together mostly people who are middle-class, middle-aged, and female. In part this was readily understandable: These are the people most likely to have the leisure and the income to come to such events, the time to attend to the things of the Spirit. The young have too much pressure placed upon them, if not by home and school, then certainly by the brainwashing of the media to get out there and get ahead in the business world. There is no time to spend on things of the Spirit. Nor is there time for the poor, who have to expend so much effort just to survive. The elderly often have the time, but we do not adapt our programs to their particular pace.

But where are the men?

If we cast our eyes around most mainline churches on an average Sunday, we meet the same reality—and more so at other parish programs. The family man might be there with his wife and children. But the others?

Do not men share the spiritual hunger that is presently surfacing with a new vigor? I believe they do.

Traditional Christian spirituality, when it seeks to speak of our deeper relationship with the Lord, has very often—following the Scriptures themselves in good part—cast the Lord in the role of the bridegroom, and the "soul" in the role of the bride. Just read again the Song of Songs and some of the many commentaries the spiritual masters have written based upon it. Undoubtedly sexual love, the marital embrace, is a wonderful image of the intimacy that the Lord wants with each of us: a complete embrace, a fruitful embrace. But for the male, so conscious of his own sexual drive, even if he is not particularly macho, such an image is not particularly inviting. He ain't no bride!

But let us take another look at the Gospel. What is the image Jesus sets forth for us there? "I have called you friends." For many men, the friendships that grew up in college years with roommates and classmates remain among the most intimate. In these friendships, made during an important time of transition, deep things have been shared—often doubts and fears as well as victories. Such friendships endure. I know that each time I pass through New York, I look forward to lunch with the men I shared with fifty years ago in Cathedral College.

Christ is the friend who is at our side, who is with us all the way, who understands everything. But more— I have been baptized into Christ. Christ is within me. Christ and I are one in some wondrous, deep way. I am Christ. I bring Christ to the world today, the everyday world in which I walk.

For men, the attractiveness of a friendship with Jesus might well be defeated by some effeminate imaging of Jesus. Such imaging is hardly compatible with the reality. This man was a carpenter, a craftsman more of the rough-hewn practical than of delicately finished work. Most of his chosen friends were a manly lot. Welcomed among them were crude fishermen, skin leathered by wind and sun, hands calloused by rope and oar; men who worked through the night and expected to face dangerous storms. His other friends included a shrewd businessman and a political activist, as well as the beloved disciple, who rested his head on Jesus breast. There was room for all types in his friendship. He was a man with great attractive power. A leader.

He was a manly man who set his face resolutely to the task, who went steadfastly toward Jerusalem. He was a physically powerful man who survived the sadistic torture of the young soldiers, and carried his cross to Calvary. He is a man worth having as a friend, worth identifying with, worth having as a model for a man's life.

Maybe the question is not where are the men? but where is the man around whom men will want to rally? Christ Jesus is a man for men, a man who offers us a wonderful, meaningful friendship. He is the man for us. Let us men gather around him.

10 | *A New Way of Listening*

LUKE 4:16–30

*When he came to Nazareth, where he had been
brought up, he went to the synagogue on the sabbath
day, as was his custom. He stood up to read, and
the scroll of the prophet Isaiah was given to him. He
unrolled the scroll and found the place where it was
written:*

*"The Spirit of the Lord is upon me,
because he has anointed me
to bring good news to the poor.
He has sent me to proclaim release to the
captives
and recovery of sight to the blind,
to let the oppressed go free,
to proclaim the year of the Lord's favor."*

*And he rolled up the scroll, gave it back to the atten-
dant, and sat down. The eyes of all in the synagogue
were fixed on him. Then he began to say to them,
"Today this scripture has been fulfilled in your
hearing." All spoke well of him and were amazed
at the gracious words that came from his mouth.
They said, "Is not this Joseph's son?" He said to
them, "Doubtless you will quote to me this proverb,
'Doctor, cure yourself!' And you will say, 'Do here
also in your hometown the things that we have heard
you did at Capernaum.'" And he said, "Truly I tell
you, no prophet is accepted in the prophet's hometown. But the truth is, there were many widows in
Israel in the time of Elijah, when the heaven was shut*

*up three years and six months, and there was a severe famine
over all the land; yet Elijah was sent to none of them except
to a widow at Zarephath in Sidon. There were also many
lepers in Israel in the time of the prophet Elisha, and none of
them was cleansed except Naaman the Syrian." When they
heard this, all in the synagogue were filled with rage. They
got up, drove him out of the town, and led him to the brow
of the hill on which their town was built, so that they might
hurl him off the cliff. But he passed through the midst of
them and went on his way.*

It was a great day for the backwater town of Nazareth.
"Can anything good come out of Nazareth?"—that
was the derisive saying making the rounds of the coun-
tryside. Well, today the hometown boy who has made
good has come home, and he is going to show his stuff.
Then they will all see what can come out of Nazareth!

We each of us have our own way of listening. We
are formed by all of our experiences to hear things in a
certain way and to hear only certain things. The people
of Nazareth listened in their own way that day, and they
missed Jesus' meaning.

What Jesus said to the people of Nazareth was not
new to them. They knew the Scriptures; that was almost
all they ever read or heard. Yet their way of listening to
Jesus was such that, when he reminded them of the widow
of Zarephath and Naaman the leper, they were filled with
indignation. They had their own way of listening to Jesus,
and this is not what they wanted to hear from him.

The result: Not only were they upset, and not only
did the meeting end in mob violence, but Jesus passed
through their midst and walked away. They completely
missed Jesus and his good news, because it did not fit
into their way of listening.

Jesus walks into our daily lives in many ways—sometimes invited, sometimes not; sometimes welcome and sometimes not so welcome. But he always comes, the bearer of the good news. Yet how often do our preconceived notions, our way of listening, prevent us from hearing him? How often do we seek to harry him out of our lives, or at least out of a particular area of our lives, because his good news isn't the good news we want to hear? Do we want a God who skips to our tune, makes things work out the way we want them to work out? Perhaps many of us, if we are truly honest, will have to answer that question in the affirmative.

Maybe it is time that, instead of making Jesus and his good news fit into our usual way of listening, we let the divine wisdom open us out into a wholly new way of listening.

How? We can try stepping aside from our own concerns, and looking at life from Jesus' perspective. It is a bit scary. It may do real violence to the way we have been listening up to now. But anyone who has really tried this can tell you, it is the way to great joy and peace.

Teaching and
Healing

11 | *As We Forgive*

LUKE 11:1–4 NIV

One day Jesus was praying in a certain place. When he finished, one of his disciples said to him, "Lord, teach us to pray, just as John taught his disciples." He said to them, "When you pray, say:
"'Father,
hallowed be your name,
your kingdom come.
Give us each day our daily bread.
Forgive us our sins,
for we also forgive everyone who sins against us.
And lead us not into temptation.'"

How often have we prayed "Forgive us our trespasses (debts, sins) as we forgive those who trespass against us." I wonder if we know what we are really saying. We are asking God to forgive us, *just as we forgive others*. In other words, if we are harboring in our hearts any unforgiveness, we are actually asking God not to forgive us but to harbor (it is hard to say this—it is so contrary to who God is) vindictiveness and unforgiveness toward us!

This was brought home to me very strongly at a Centering Prayer workshop I was conducting a dozen years ago. One of the participants came up to me and said plaintively, "I cannot pray the Lord's prayer." She understood what it said. And she was harboring in her heart—humanly speaking, very understandably—unforgiveness against the young man who had randomly murdered her fine young son as he slept. I am happy to report that, by God's grace, this good woman did rise to forgiveness, and now has a very loving relationship with that young murderer, who is in prison.

Heroic—yes! Whenever I pray the Lord's prayer and arrive at those words: "as [I] forgive those who have trespassed against [me]," I quickly add within: "Lord, with all my heart, as best I can, I forgive everyone everything." That is easy enough said when some wound is not open and burning, or festering deep within. Yet forgiveness is not always easily come by. Sometimes anger and resentment are nursed into us with our mothers' milk, as we see so painfully in places like Northern Ireland, among the tribes of Central Africa, and in so many other places in our poor wounded world. Many of us, if we are honest, know that unforgiveness has been rooted deep within our own hearts by the prevailing prejudices of our family, community, church, or race.

Fortunately, today there is a growing realization that forgiveness is the way to go—in fact, the only way for us, whether as individuals, as nations, or as peoples. At one time we might have been amazed to hear that the Templeton Foundation has given a ten-million-dollar grant for forgiveness research; that Robert Enright has founded a Forgiveness Institute in Madison, Wisconsin; and that Stanford University offers a course called The Art and Science of Forgiveness. Medical and psychological studies certainly confirm how much harm we do to ourselves when we do not forgive.

But forgiveness is not easy. Forgiving includes facing up to the fact that we have been hurt—something many of us don't like to acknowledge. It is humbling to admit that someone can hurt us. Then we have to give up the grudge. And in the end, we have to choose to show mercy. Scripture tells us that mercy is God's greatest work (see, for example, Psalm 103). In love, we respond to what is good; in mercy, we respond to what is not good and seek to make it good.

Jesus has told us: "Apart from me you can do nothing" (John 15:5). That certainly applies here. When we become aware of any unforgiveness in our hearts, we need first to turn to the Lord for help as we begin the process of letting go of the grudge and choosing mercy. For us it may seem impossible—and it is, but we can do all things through him who strengthens us (Philippians 4:13).

Before we utter the Lord's prayer again, let us search our hearts and seek to clear them of any resentment or anger, or even unfriendliness, so that we can say to the Lord: "Lord, I forgive everyone with all my heart as best I can."

12 | *Gratitude and Generosity*

You have heard that it was said, "You shall love your neighbor and hate your enemy." But I say to you, Love your enemies and pray for those who persecute you, so that you may be children of your Father in heaven; for he makes his sun rise on the evil and on the good, and sends rain on the righteous and on the unrighteous. For if you love those who love you, what reward do you have? Do not even the tax collectors do the same? And if you greet only your brothers and sisters, what more are you doing than others? Do not even the Gentiles do the same? Be perfect, therefore, as your heavenly Father is perfect.

Most us at a very early age were taught to say thank you. I can still hear my mother's voice prompting: "What do you say?"

It is very important, of course, to learn to express our gratitude for the goodness and kindness of others toward us. Unfortunately we were not always taught to express our gratitude to God regularly for the many things God gives us and does for us. I have been in many homes where grace was said before the meal, asking God to bless it—and the fact that this at least is being done is a good thing—but there was no pause for thanksgiving after the meal. Maybe the folks didn't think it was a meal worth thanking God for! But if we think for a moment of what most of our brothers and sisters on this planet are having this day, we would indeed realize we have reason to say thank you for whatever we get to eat.

It is good and important that parents teach their children thanksgiving, and they can only do this at the child's level of development. But what often happens is that parents go no further as the child grows in capacity to learn. Thus we are left with the sense that a perfunctory or ritualistic thank you is enough. How often do we say thank you without a real sense of appreciation and gratitude toward the person and for what we have received? Likewise, how perfunctory and ritualistic is our giving thanks to the Lord, even if we do it regularly?

Some spiritual traditions stress mindfulness and have exercises to promote this. This is a wonderful thing. It invites us to live at a more fully human level of consciousness—a reflective consciousness worthy of a person who has received from God a mind and a heart capable of true and sincere appreciation and gratitude. It takes time to arrive at this level of humanness. We can begin to move in this direction by taking time regularly to reflect on the gifts of God that we receive directly or through others at every moment of life: for starters, that we can breathe and for the air we breathe. Since God gives to us without ceasing, twenty-four hours a day, would it not be reasonable to take a minute at the end of each meal to say thank you, and to take a couple of minutes as we crawl into bed at night to reflect on the blessings of the day?

Now I want to take a minute to look at this from the other side: our own expectation of being thanked. When we do something for someone, even when it is in the line of duty, we rightly expect some sort of appreciation and expression of gratitude. At times we feel hurt, if not angry, when what we consider due thanksgiving is not forthcoming. What does this tell us of ourselves? We might say, it says I was brought up properly and learned to say thanks, and that there is something wrong with this other person. All this might be true. But I think it also might help us to realize that our giving, our service, was not all that magnanimous or altruistic, that we were acting with a certain amount of self-concern, looking for something in return, be it but some affirmation of our own worth and accomplishment.

Jesus challenges us to be perfect like our heavenly Father—for we are made in God's image and our happiness lies in this likeness—who lets his sun shine on the good and evil alike, who lets his rain fall on the just and unjust without distinction. God does not expect to be thanked by those who are evil and unjust. If God wants us to be grateful, it is not because God gets anything out of it. It is because thanksgiving means we are in touch with the reality of God's beneficence and will find joy in this.

When we act expecting others to be grateful and to express their gratitude to our own satisfaction, we often enough end up unhappy, for their appreciation and thanksgiving will rarely be as profuse as we had hoped. If, on the other hand, we look for appreciation and thanks because we want the other's joy to be fuller, our joy in giving will not be diminished even if they express no gratitude at all. We will experience a certain compassionate sorrow at their loss, but we won't need to be assured of our worth by the affirmation of others. Our goodness and generosity flow from the abundant Source within, and we can be joyfully grateful when we realize this.

As St. Paul says, "In all circumstances give thanks" (1 Thessalonians 5:18 NAB).

13 | *We Piped You a Tune*

MATTHEW 11:16–19 NAB

"To what shall I compare this generation? It is like children who sit in the marketplaces and call to one another,

> *'We played the flute for you, but you did not dance,*
> *we sang a dirge but you did not mourn.'*

For John came neither eating nor drinking, and they said, 'He is possessed by a demon.' The Son of Man came eating and drinking, and they said, 'Look, he is a glutton and a drunkard, a friend of tax collectors and sinners.' But wisdom is vindicated by her works."

One day when our Lord was speaking to the crowds, he used what at first hearing seems like a curious analogy. What is this generation like? he asked. They are like children playing in the square, chanting: "We piped you a tune and you did not dance; we sang you a dirge and you did not wail."

What is Jesus trying to tell us here?

Since becoming abbot, one thing I have learned. Everyone in the monastery might have a vow of obedience to obey the abbot, but in practice, everyone expects the abbot to obey him.

And that, I believe, is what Jesus is talking about here. We pipe our tune and we expect God to dance. We ask for something in prayer and we expect God immediately to get to work and do exactly what we want. If he doesn't, we whine: God doesn't listen to me. God doesn't hear my prayer. God doesn't care about me. Or we even go so far as to say: There is no God.

But every parent knows that at times the appropriate answer is, quite simply: No!

I remember one evening in my brother's home. He has eight children, and we were all gathered around the table enjoying a wonderful meal. Suddenly little Neil, three at the time, caught sight of the bright shiny handle of the carving knife. That certainly looked like something worth having, something fun to play with. As he reached for it, his watchful mother was quicker. She immediately moved it out of his reach. Then he began to whine: You are an old meany. You won't let me have what I want. After a bit, mother placated him with some cake and ice cream.

Little Neil was looking for happiness. That is what we are all looking for. And he thought happiness lay in playing with the shiny carving knife. He might have been happy with it for a minute or two, but then he might have cut off his hand and been unhappy the rest of his life. Often enough we think that what we are asking God for is surely the way to happiness for us or for our loved ones. But in fact in the great plan of God, who sees all, the passing happiness, as good as it may appear, might lead us to eternal unhappiness. So in love, God says: No.

We piped and God did not dance. He was busy preparing better things for us, sources of more lasting and deeper happiness.

I am sure most of us, if we pause and look back over our lives, can think of times when we asked for a certain thing from God and his answer seemed to be no. He seemed just to ignore us. But then later we saw that it was good that our prayer was not answered the way that we had wanted it answered. I am sure that there have been many times in my life when God has said no and I have not yet realized what a blessing that answer was or will be.

Yes, let us pipe. Let us pray aplenty. But let us not be so childish as to expect the Lord God, who is all wise and loving, always to dance to our tune.

14 | Who Touched Me?

LUKE 8:40–48 NAB

When Jesus returned, the crowd welcomed him, for they were all waiting for him. And a man named Jairus, an official of the synagogue, came forward. He fell at the feet of Jesus and begged him to come to his house, because he had an only daughter, about twelve years old, and she was dying. As he went, the crowds almost crushed him. And a woman afflicted with hemorrhages for twelve years, who [had spent her whole livelihood on doctors and] was unable to be cured by anyone, came up behind him and touched the tassel of his cloak. Immediately her bleeding stopped. Jesus then asked, "Who touched me?" While all were denying it, Peter said, "Master, the crowds are pushing and pressing in upon you." But Jesus said, "Someone has touched me; for I know that power has gone out from me." When the woman realized that she had not escaped notice, she came forward trembling. Falling down before him, she explained in the presence of all the people why she had touched him and how she had been healed immediately. He said to her, "Daughter, your faith has saved you; go in peace."

We all love to travel, to see new things, hear new sounds, smell new smells, touch and be touched by more and more of the array of this wondrous world our most munificent Creator has given us. All this is good. But some of us enjoy these experiences primarily on the material level of being, as if only the sense perceptions were real or important; as if we could be affected only through physical experience. By contrast, the fully alive person knows that the most meaningful contacts are made at another level of being.

In this Gospel passage a distraught father comes to Jesus. His child is dying. Jesus agrees to come immediately. As he sets out, a curious, jostling crowd pushes through the narrow way along with him. He and his disciples are being knocked about from every side. Suddenly Jesus stops and asks: "Who touched me?"

Peter in his usual obtuse way responds: How can you ask, who touched me? Everyone is touching us. Everybody is pushing us about.

Yes, physically they were being touched by multitudes. But only one person had touched Jesus in the fullness of her humanity, with spirit and faith as well as body. And she received her reward: a complete cure.

The increase of material contact—the jostling crowd, the over-scheduled business day, relentless demands on our time—almost necessarily means a decrease in spiritual contact, unless all our contact is grounded in contemplation and the operation of the gifts of the Spirit that are set free to work in our lives by contemplative prayer.

Mobs may have been pushing Jesus this way and that, but he did not miss the one contact that was Spirit-filled. For he was a man who spent whole nights in prayer.

We have seen this in our own time in Mother Teresa of Calcutta. As her reputation grew, she was more and more mobbed as she moved about. But a moment in her eyes remains an unforgettable experience; anyone who has had the experience can bear witness to that. When one saw oneself in her eyes, one saw oneself as Christ. This phenomenon didn't just happen. Mother habitually spent four hours in prayer before she set out on her demanding daily tasks, and she asked all her nuns to do the same. From that prayer she went out to bring Jesus to others. And she found him wherever he was, in other people and in other things.

Years ago I visited the Acropolis. Very early in the morning I climbed up the rugged ascent, hoping to enjoy its beauty quietly before the crowds began to come. Soon enough the tourist buses arrived to disgorge their curious and harried travelers who rushed about snapping pictures, hardly taking a moment to look and see and experience the wonders they were busily recording on film. When they got home they would have difficulty remembering just what each picture was, and the pictures would fail to summon up any real meaning. They might just as well have stayed home and collected postcards. But down below, on a rise next to the Acropolis called the Areopagus where St Paul is said to have preached, a few walked about quietly and another few sat in meditation, some with Bible in hand. For these it would be an unforgettable experience. Certainly I have never forgotten it.

Grounded in Reality, we do not need to go out and about to find meaning. It is all here within. And when we go out, we find the same Reality. Whether within or without, it fills us with presence, joy, and completeness. Grounded, we can truly touch the lives of others and be touched by them.

15 | *Eat My Flesh*

*Then the Jews began to complain about him because
he said, "I am the bread that came down from
heaven." They were saying, "Is not this Jesus, the son
of Joseph, whose father and mother we know? How
can he now say, 'I have come down from heaven'?"
Jesus answered them, "Do not complain among
yourselves. No one can come to me unless drawn by
the Father who sent me; and I will raise that person
up on the last day. It is written in the prophets, 'And
they shall all be taught by God.' Everyone who has
heard and learned from the Father comes to me. Not
that anyone has seen the Father except the one who
is from God; he has seen the Father. Very truly, I
tell you, whoever believes has eternal life. I am the
bread of life. Your ancestors ate the manna in the
wilderness, and they died. This is the bread that
comes down from heaven, so that one may eat of it
and not die. I am the living bread that came down
from heaven. Whoever eats of this bread will live
forever; and the bread that I will give for the life of
the world is my flesh."*

*The Jews then disputed among themselves, saying,
"How can this man give us his flesh to eat?" So Jesus
said to them, "Very truly, I tell you, unless you eat
the flesh of the Son of Man and drink his blood,
you have no life in you. Those who eat my flesh and
drink my blood have eternal life, and I will raise
them up on the last day; for my flesh is true food*

and my blood is true drink. Those who eat my flesh and drink my blood abide in me, and I in them. Just as the living Father sent me, and I live because of the Father, so whoever eats me will live because of me. This is the bread that came down from heaven, not like that which your ancestors ate, and they died. But the one who eats this bread will live forever."

"Stop murmuring," says the Lord to the crowd. Well, I think they might have some cause to murmur. This man has just said to them, "eat my flesh . . ." Eat his flesh!

I am afraid we have got so used to the idea of eating the Lord's flesh in sacramental form in Holy Communion that we cannot appreciate how barbaric this statement seemed to his hearers.

The day before, after a long day of preaching and teaching, Jesus had fed these people with all the bread and fish they wanted. All enjoyed the feast, but many had not awakened sufficiently to the fact that it was a feast miraculously provided, a sign of God's confirmation of the teacher. One thing they knew. This man could feed them. And so they pursued him.

When the people caught up with Jesus, seeking more to eat, Jesus chided them. "You are seeking the bread that perishes." He offered them something better: the bread for eternal life—his own flesh. This was too much for them. They murmured against him, and in the end, most went away.

In offering them—and us—his flesh, albeit in sacramental form, Jesus is inviting them and us to rise to a higher level of consciousness.

When we eat ordinary food, the food is assimilated by us and raised to a higher level of being as it is integrated into human life. But when we eat this holy food, the flesh of the Lord, the food we eat is not turned into us. We are turned into the food; we are made into Christ.

In truth, we cannot worthily eat the flesh of Christ, enter into communion—"union with" Christ's flesh—unless we are willing to be one flesh with him. That means being ready to offer our flesh, our comfort, our very lives, for the salvation and well-being of all our sisters and brothers, just as Jesus did. Our communion is not true if we are not disposed to give ourselves for others. When Jesus says, "Unless you eat the flesh of the Son of Man and drink his blood, you have no life in you," he is proclaiming in other words his basic statement: "Whoever does not carry the cross and follow me cannot be my disciple" (Luke 14:27).

Communion—union with Christ through eating his flesh and drinking his blood in the sacrament—is a true life-giving sign only when we are ready to be one with Jesus in his gift of self for the salvation of us all.

16 | *Who Do You Say . . . ?*

MATTHEW 16:13–23

Now when Jesus came into the district of Caesarea Philippi, he asked his disciples, "Who do people say that the Son of Man is?" And they said, "Some say John the Baptist, but others Elijah, and still others Jeremiah or one of the prophets." He said to them, "But who do you say that I am?" Simon Peter answered, "You are the Messiah, the Son of the living God." And Jesus answered him, "Blessed are you, Simon son of Jonah! For flesh and blood has not revealed this to you, but my Father in heaven. And I tell you, you are Peter, and on this rock I will build my church, and the gates of Hades will not prevail against it. I will give you the keys of the kingdom of heaven, and whatever you bind on earth will be bound in heaven, and whatever you loose on earth will be loosed in heaven." Then he sternly ordered the disciples not to tell anyone that he was the Messiah.

From that time on, Jesus began to show his disciples that he must go to Jerusalem and undergo great suffering at the hands of the elders and chief priests and scribes, and be killed, and on the third day be raised. And Peter took him aside and began to rebuke him, saying, "God forbid it, Lord! This must never happen to you." But he turned and said to Peter, "Get behind me, Satan! You are a stumbling block to me; for you are setting your mind not on divine things but on human things."

The Gospels are full of wonderful little stories, and this is one of my favorites.

Jesus had finally escaped the crowds and was able to withdraw into a fairly quiet spot with his Twelve. It would be an opportunity to instruct them and lead them into a deeper understanding of who he is and what his mission involved. They were far in the north of the Jewish territory, in a region called Caesarea Philippi.

Jesus began by asking them a simple question: Who do folks say that I am? The Twelve were quick to respond, each one joining in—no risk here. John the Baptizer, said one. Elijah. Jeremiah. One of the prophets.

When they had exhausted their repertoire, Jesus again spoke: "Who do *you* say that I am?"

The great silence.

Now he was putting them on the spot. Now it was time to take a stand, to make a declaration. (Before you read on, why don't you pause for a moment to let Jesus look you straight in the eye and ask you: "Who do you say that I am?" What do *you* answer?)

For once, Peter came through. This braggart, whose mouth often got ahead of his brain, said without hesitation, "You are the Messiah, the Son of the living God." It is hard for us to appreciate fully this response, to understand what *Messiah* meant to these men who had lived all their lives among an oppressed and humiliated people. The Messiah was the liberator, the one who would vindicate them, the one who would trample down their enemies and would make them once again a great nation.

But Peter didn't stop with *Messiah*. Indeed, he was led on to say much more: "You are the Son of the living God."

We would be inclined to say that Peter didn't really know what he was saying when he made this magnificent profession of faith—except that Jesus immediately not only affirmed it but revealed its source. "Blessed are you, Simon son of Jonah! For flesh and blood has not revealed this to you, but my Father in heaven." Not any human spirit but Holy Spirit acting within this man brought him to a new, exalted level of consciousness. It was a faith so solid that Jesus could build his church upon it.

We all want and need such a faith. But we all know our all-too-human weaknesses. We do not want to let them deter us. For look what happened on this wondrous occasion in Caesarea Philippi.

Jesus went on instructing his chosen ones, foretelling how his church would be built upon Peter. Then he foretold the path that would lead to the birth of that church, and it was not a very pleasant one. He would be betrayed, brutalized, and hung on a cross to die. And he would rise again.

Peter's rock-like faith was not ready for all of this. His humanity rose up in revulsion. This was not his messianic dream. Such degradation was not to be tolerated. "God forbid it, Lord! This must never happen to you." And this man, whom Jesus had just praised as the recipient of divine enlightenment, was now called a "Satan," an adversary: "Get behind me, Satan! You are an obstacle to me. You are thinking not as God does, but as human beings do" (verse 23, NAB). Yes, even when we are illuminated by Holy Spirit in one area, even a very fundamental area, the human spirit and even other spirits can still hold their corner within us. God has not finished his work in us.

We need the rock-like faith of Peter, who would eventually go all the way for Jesus. We can ask for it and expect it as a gift from our most good and gracious Father in heaven. But even as we receive this precious gift, we should not be surprised to find our human spirit that has been twisted by sin still making its claims. This is one of the reasons why we need each day to turn to the Gospels, to *lectio,* meeting the Lord and letting him, through his powerful word, enlighten our minds and hearts, driving out the deceiving spirit of this passing world.

With our rock-like faith we can come to Jesus in the Gospels, the living Word, and come to know the way and the truth, and find the fullness of life.

17 | *The Good Housewife*

LUKE 15:3–10

So he told them this parable: "Which one of you, having a hundred sheep and losing one of them, does not leave the ninety-nine in the wilderness and go after the one that is lost until he finds it? When he has found it, he lays it on his shoulders and rejoices. And when he comes home, he calls together his friends and neighbors, saying to them, 'Rejoice with me, for I have found my sheep that was lost.' Just so, I tell you, there will be more joy in heaven over one sinner who repents than over ninety-nine righteous persons who need no repentance.

"Or what woman having ten silver coins, if she loses one of them, does not light a lamp, sweep the house, and search carefully until she finds it? When she has found it, she calls together her friends and neighbors, saying, 'Rejoice with me, for I have found the coin that I had lost.'"

"Male and female he created them," we read in the first chapter of Genesis—and ever since, it has been a real challenge to us. Especially now that we have arrived at that point in the evolution of human consciousness where we understand that men and women are truly equal, both coming forth from the loving creative hand of God.

Let us be honest. Equality scares some of us men—right down to our little toes. Oh, we come up with all sorts of reasons for the way things have been: theological, psychological, anthropological, physiological, and all the other "logicals"—few of which reasons are logical at all!

Jesus foresaw our struggles. It is amazing. All through the centuries, no matter what question has arisen, there are keys to the answer in the Gospels. If only we look.

When Jesus depicted himself as the Good Shepherd (an image we all so love), he immediately added another image of himself: the Good Housewife. It is noteworthy: for all the times we see the Good Shepherd imaged in art, how often do we see the Good Housewife? And yet is this image not closer to us? How many of us have ever lost or will ever lose a sheep? At most we might lose a cat or dog. But all of us have lost some little thing around the house and have had to go hunting for it in drawers and under things.

How close this womanly image of Jesus is to us. The next time you lose something and find yourself poking around your home, think of the Good Housewife and know that God, who values you far more than you value what you are looking for, is ever looking for you, your love, your attention, your nearness to him in love.

Jesus was not afraid to image himself as a woman, for he was a real man. He knew full well that he, one with his Father and Spirit, made humankind male and female. Both are made in the image of God. Male and female are fully equal. How good it will be when we can reclaim that truth, and rejoice in our true equality as sons and daughters of God.

18 | *The Better Portion*

Now as they went on their way, he entered a certain village, where a woman named Martha welcomed him into her home. She had a sister named Mary, who sat at the Lord's feet and listened to what he was saying. But Martha was distracted by her many tasks; so she came to him and asked, "Lord, do you not care that my sister has left me to do all the work by myself? Tell her to help me." But the Lord answered her, "Martha, Martha, you are worried and distracted by many things; there is need of only one thing. Mary has chosen the better part, which will not be taken away from her."

Those of us who have listened to this particular passage many times through the years are more used to hearing "Mary has chosen the *best* part", which leaves us with a somewhat different sense of the Lord's words. Actually, a literal translation of Luke's text would be that Mary has chosen "the good part."

In some translations, the word here translated "part" is given as "portion"—"Mary has chosen the good portion," says the Revised Standard Version. The word *portion* invites us to think of a richly laden table set out before us.

Some justify the use of the comparative *better* here because they understand our Lord to be comparing two ways of life: the active service of Martha and the contemplative presence of Mary. But I hardly think that is what the Lord is about here. He is pointing out the goodness of the portion Mary is choosing at this moment, a portion we all want to choose and enjoy as part of our Christ-life, even if that life is spent mostly in service. *Better* or *best* might be justifiable translations from a linguistic standpoint, but they perhaps go beyond what our Lord is asserting when he tells us that Mary has chosen the good part.

We are all by baptism called to live the Christ life. That is a life with many facets, as is each of our own lives. Even those who, in responding to a divine invitation, have chosen the contemplative life will readily tell us that their days are not spent wholly sitting at the Lord's feet, like Mary in this particular instance. They too take part in humankind's primal penance: to earn their living by the sweat of their brow. They too find many calls to serve their brothers and sisters, even within the cloister.

On the other hand, the enjoyment of the contemplative "portion" is not reserved exclusively to these few. Indeed, the Second Vatican Council made it very clear that all who have been baptized into Christ are meant to share in this.

If our Lord is reprimanding Martha, or making a comparison between her present attitude and Mary's, it is that Martha is "worried and distracted by many things." Rather than going joyfully and wholeheartedly about her chosen portion, that of serving the Lord and his friends, she is anxious. She needs to hear St. Peter's words: "Cast all your anxiety on him, because he cares for you" (1 Peter 5:7). Moreover, Martha is allowing herself to be upset because her sister, probably a younger sister, is choosing a different portion, and one that seems preferable. In our love, we want to rejoice whenever each of our sisters and brothers finds the good portion, the one that is best for her or him.

We all need to hear the Lord's word here: The contemplative portion, time spent sitting quietly with the Lord, is a good portion. There is a Martha part in all of us that seeks to drive us on and not allow us to enjoy this. On the other hand, medical and psychological practice today affirms more and more strongly our great need of such quiet, healing time, as we live in such a frenetic world. The tensions mount in us and will lead to hypertension, heart problems, and other ills, if we are not able to release them. We do release them to some extent through sleep and routine exercise, but a contemplative sort of meditation is the best way to free ourselves from anxiety.

However true this is, however healing contemplative prayer may be, it is much more than a remedy. Letting everything else go, and letting ourselves be inundated by the inflow of divine love, is not only healing; it satisfies the deepest aspirations of our being. It is the realization of our deepest longings. It calls us forth to a transforming love that adds quality and depth to all the rest of our lives. It leads to the fulfillment of who we are and all that we are called to be. We are meant to dine regularly on this "good portion."

19 | *I Want to See!*

MARK 10:46–52 NAB

They came to Jericho. And as he was leaving Jericho with his disciples and a sizable crowd, Bartimaeus, a blind man, the son of Timaeus, sat by the roadside begging. On hearing that it was Jesus of Nazareth, he began to cry out and say, "Jesus, son of David, have pity on me." And many rebuked him, telling him to be silent. But he kept calling out all the more, "Son of David, have pity on me." Jesus stopped and said, "Call him." So they called the blind man, saying to him, "Take courage; get up, he is calling you." He threw aside his cloak, sprang up, and came to Jesus. Jesus said to him in reply, "What do you want me to do for you?" The blind man replied to him, "Master, I want to see." Jesus told him, "Go your way; your faith has saved you." Immediately he received his sight and followed him on the way.

We are all probably familiar with the story of Bartimaeus, the blind man at the gates of Jericho. How long he had been there begging we do not know: weeks, months, years, a lifetime. There was evidently another blind man there with him (see the similar story in Matthew 20:30–34). Such companionship must have been a great comfort.

And now rumors were spreading. There was a great healer in the land. He had actually opened the eyes of a blind man up in Galilee. Indeed, he had fed thousands in the wilderness, calmed the sea, changed water into wine, and even raised a dead man to life at the gates of Nain. How the two talked among themselves about all this. Oh, if only they could get to him. Or if he would come their way.

Then one day there was a great hubbub. As curious as any, Bartimaeus inquired what it was all about. The healer was coming out of the city, he was told. The healer! Here! With all his might he cried out: "Jesus, son of David, have pity on me." Those nearby tried to silence him. They wanted to hear what the healer was saying, not the cries of this blind beggar.

Then it happened. "Take courage; get up, he is calling you," someone in the crowd said. Bartimaeus threw aside his cloak. We can hardly appreciate what a significant act this was. The cloak was a most prized possession in this society. For the poor it was a bed, a cover, security against the elements. The law provided that if one gave his cloak as surety against a loan, it had to be returned to him each night so he could sleep in it. Bartimaeus let his go, let everything go, and with eagerness stumbled his way through a helping crowd to the healer.

We have heard the question before. They were the first words Jesus is recorded as having said to his disciples, that day when Andrew and John ran up behind him at the banks of the Jordan: "What do you want?" (John 1:35–40). This remains Jesus' word to each of us: "What do you want?"

He will give us what we want: Ask and you shall receive (Matthew 7:7–8). And it is here precisely that this poor blind beggar is a model for us. "Master, I want to see."

The Lord will give us whatever we want. The problem is that we, who want happiness (for that is what we are made for—to share the divine happiness), do not know wherein lies our happiness. We who have been blinded by sin—our own and those of a sinful world that seeks to entice us into all sorts of false happiness—cannot see clearly. "Master, I want to see." I want to see what is necessary to my true happiness.

The ending of this story is significant. Jesus heals Bartimaeus and tells him to go. And then the evangelist tells us that Bartimaeus followed Jesus "on the way." Bartimaeus not only got the gift of physical sight, so precious indeed, but he received a true illumination. He now saw that his way was to follow Jesus, that Jesus is the way. In Jesus we find the way, the truth, and eternal life—all that our deepest being seeks.

Today, if we but have ears to hear, Jesus says to you and to me: "What do you want?" And if we have the wisdom of this poor blind beggar, we too will cry out: "Master, I want to see."

20 | *The Importance of Resurrection*

MARK 12:18–27

Some Sadducees, who say there is no resurrection, came to him and asked him a question, saying, "Teacher, Moses wrote for us that 'if a man's brother dies, leaving a wife but no child, the man shall marry the widow and raise up children for his brother.' There were seven brothers; the first married and, when he died, left no children; and the second married her and died, leaving no children; and the third likewise; none of the seven left children. Last of all the woman herself died. In the resurrection whose wife will she be? For the seven had married her."

Jesus said to them, "Is not this the reason you are wrong, that you know neither the scriptures nor the power of God? For when they rise from the dead, they neither marry nor are given in marriage, but are like angels in heaven. And as for the dead being raised, have you not read in the book of Moses, in the story about the bush, how God said to him, 'I am the God of Abraham, the God of Isaac, and the God of Jacob'? He is God not of the dead, but of the living; you are quite wrong."

Mark's Gospel tells us that one day a group of Sadducees approached Jesus. In constant contention with the Pharisees, these men held that there was no resurrection. They were hoping to align Jesus with their position or at least trap him so that he could not accept the opposite. So they brought the fabricated story of a woman who successively married seven brothers and buried each of them. If there is a resurrection, whose wife is she?

I marvel at Jesus' patience. One group after another came at him, each making futile and rather stupid attempts to make him look bad. It was enough to try the patience of a saint, and maybe even that of this maker of saints, who deigned to be like us in all but sin.

In any case, on this particular occasion his answer was exceptionally forceful: "Is not this the reason you are wrong, that you know neither the Scriptures nor the power of God? . . . You are quite wrong." A literal translation of the Greek would yield an even more forceful response.

We might ask ourselves if Jesus might say of us also: "You are quite wrong." Is the way we are living our daily lives "quite wrong" because we do not understand the Scriptures or because we do not really believe in the power of God? Does the revelation of Jesus, given to us in the Gospels and Epistles, really lead and guide us in the way we live? Or are we following other, lesser lights that are not wholly informed by truth? Do we look to the Scriptures daily for guidance?

Here Jesus is pointing to the resurrection. St. Paul has told us: "If there is no resurrection of the dead, then Christ has not been raised; and if Christ has not been raised, then our proclamation has been in vain and your faith has been in vain. If Christ be not risen, then our faith is in vain" (1 Corinthians 15:13–14).

But the resurrection is not just an event that proves the authenticity of the Lord and his teaching. It is important that we keep our eyes on the risen Lord. Here we see the hope of our lives: We too shall rise.

This reality enlightens our days and helps us to keep things in perspective. In view of the eternal happiness that lies ahead for us, how great is the sorrow or pain of today, be it the pain of an hour, a week, a month, a decade, or many decades? What lies ahead for us is eternal, unending, everlasting—joy unlimited. "As it is written, 'What no eye has seen, nor ear heard, nor the human heart conceived, what God has prepared for those who love him'—these things God has revealed to us through the Spirit; for the Spirit searches everything, even the depths of God" (1 Corinthians 2:9–10). The risen Christ in glory at the right hand of the Father, the sight that filled the martyr Stephen with joy even as he was stoned to death, gives a whole new meaning to our lives.

But there is more. St. Paul has also reminded us that we who are baptized into Christ are to fill up what is wanting in the passion of Christ (see Colossians 1:24). Our sufferings united to those of Christ bring salvation and the joy of the resurrection to ourselves, our loved ones, and the whole needy world. This realization can turn pain and suffering into joy. What a privilege it is for us to be called to suffer redemptively with Christ. Not that suffering in itself is good. It is a consequence of sin and the abuse of nature. But it offers us an opportunity to grow in selfless and self-giving love. It is love that matters.

Keeping our eyes on the Risen One, we can go through our sufferings and everything else in this passing life with hope, joy, and expectation.

21 | *The Good Samaritan*

Out of the Box

LUKE 10:25–37

*Just then a lawyer stood up to test Jesus. "Teacher,"
he said, "what must I do to inherit eternal life?" He
said to him, "What is written in the law? What do
you read there?" He answered, "You shall love the
Lord your God with all your heart, and with all your
soul, and with all your strength, and with all your
mind; and your neighbor as yourself." And he said to
him, "You have given the right answer; do this, and
you will live."*

*But wanting to justify himself, he asked Jesus,
"And who is my neighbor?" Jesus replied, "A man
was going down from Jerusalem to Jericho, and fell
into the hands of robbers, who stripped him, beat
him, and went away, leaving him half dead. Now by
chance a priest was going down that road; and when
he saw him, he passed by on the other side. So likewise a Levite, when he came to the place and saw
him, passed by on the other side. But a Samaritan
while traveling came near him; and when he saw
him, he was moved with pity. He went to him and
bandaged his wounds, having poured oil and wine
on them. Then he put him on his own animal,
brought him to an inn, and took care of him. The
next day he took out two denarii, gave them to the
innkeeper, and said, 'Take care of him; and when
I come back, I will repay you whatever more you
spend.' Which of these three, do you think, was a
neighbor to the man who fell into the hands of the*

robbers?" He said, "The one who showed him mercy."
Jesus said to him, "Go and do likewise."

Yes, they knew. Everybody knew. Those Samaritans, they were just plain bad. You could heap on them every negative adjective in your vocabulary, and you would still not be going too far. A Samaritan was a Samaritan, and that was that. End of discussion.

Then Jesus began his story. And they were caught up in it. They knew the road down to Jericho. They had gone that way many times, or they knew people who had made that journey. It was dangerous. Those brigands were something else. They would jump out on a solitary traveler and beat him for all he was worth. They would strip him bare, even taking his loincloth. There was just no mercy.

Yes, of course the priest passed by. What else could you expect from a priest? After all, he could not chance getting ritually unclean. And so, too, the Levite, the glorified altar boy. Then there was the Samaritan. He didn't have to worry about ritual uncleanness. He stepped in. He did what needed to be done: cleaned the wounds, bound them as best he could, loaded the man onto his donkey . . .

Before they knew it, they were caught (I can just imagine Jesus smiling to himself: Gotcha!). Here was a Samaritan doing what was good, caring for a fellow human in his need—and a Jew at that. Their box was shattered. A *good* Samaritan!

We have perhaps heard the story too often. It is too well known to us to have its intended impact. Moreover, "Samaritan" in no way carries for us the whole weight of centuries of animosity and prejudice. Perhaps we need to try something like the good Arab, or the good Jew, or the good gay, or the good fundamentalist, or the good panhandler. Or maybe even the good abortionist!

Actually Jesus never called the man the good Samaritan. That is our labeling. In fact he did not evaluate the person at all. He only asked: Who was a neighbor? He did not condone nor condemn Samaritan ignorance or error, prejudice or atrocities. But charity covers a multitude of sins.

We all tend to put others in boxes. We may not be so blatant. We may not look down on a whole group (though the American superiority complex is well known among people in other countries). In our case it may be Uncle Fred, or cousin Lily, or the boss, or the local parish priest that we have boxed in. We know all about them. We know what to expect. We are glad we are not like them.

But who really is in the box? We think they are, but they go merrily on their way. And we are left in a box of our own making. It prevents us from ever discovering the beauty that God has created in those people. It prevents them from ever making the contribution to our lives that God intended our contact with them to bring to us. We are the prisoners of our prejudices, not the persons whom we seek to imprison in our narrowness and pride.

Let's trash all our boxes, and know the freedom of allowing every person to relate to us in all their beauty and giftedness. And let us not forget the word of our all-good Master: "Truly I tell you, just as you did it to one of the least of these who are members of my family, you did it to me" (Matthew 25:40). It is he, however deeply disguised, who comes to us in every human person.

22 | *The Good Samaritan*

Love in Action

1 JOHN 3:11, 16–20

For this is the message you have heard from the beginning, that we should love one another. . . . We know love by this, that he laid down his life for us—and we ought to lay down our lives for one another. How does God's love abide in anyone who has the world's goods and sees a brother or sister in need and yet refuses help?

Little children, let us love, not in word or speech, but in truth and action. And by this we will know that we are from the truth and will reassure our hearts before him whenever our hearts condemn us; for God is greater than our hearts, and he knows everything.

He looked like a typical collegian, the more athletic type—brush cut, bulging muscles. And yet as he shared his story he could not keep the tears from coming. And mine mingled with his.

The story had started five years earlier. Joe was coming home from school. Ahead of him he saw a classmate, one he knew only by sight. The fellow was struggling with quite a load of stuff, and suddenly he lost the battle. Books, sneakers, athletic equipment all went in different directions.

Joe ran up and helped him retrieve some of the straying items. It was too much to load on one man, so Joe walked along with him, carrying his share. He learned that his classmate's name was Li.

When they reached Li's house, Joe was invited in for a Coke. The two boys started talking, and it was three hours later when they finally said goodbye.

As they moved toward graduation from junior high, they would stop to chat once in a while. They both ended up at the same high school, and the casual acquaintance continued.

Then a month before Joe told me the story, as the two young men were standing around waiting for the graduation ceremonies to begin, Li came over to Joe and said: "I want to thank you."

"For what?" Joe asked.

"For today, for so much more, for my life."

Joe didn't understand, and his face showed it. Li went on: "Did you ever wonder, that afternoon when you helped me, why I was carrying so much stuff home from school? Well, I had cleaned out my locker because I didn't want to leave the job to anyone else. I had gotten a bottle of sleeping pills, and I was going to commit suicide that night. But then you came along, and we spent three good hours together. When you left, I thought: If I had killed myself I would never have had these three good hours—and maybe many more like them. So I threw the pills away, thanks to you."

As Joe finished the story, the tears flowed down his cheeks. He didn't have to tell me that they had flowed also that day as he and Li hugged.

A Good Samaritan story? Yes, indeed. And maybe it says something about assisted suicide, too. A little bit of time and attention can change a world. It is hard to make that time when we have an agenda, things to do, plans to carry out. But maybe, remembering Joe and Li, next time we see someone who needs help we will respond, letting our own plans go. It may not seem like a life-and-death situation—but who knows? One thing our faith tells us: anyone who needs our help is the Lord.

23 | *The Good Samaritan*

No Room for Prejudice

GALATIONS 3:23–29

Now before faith came, we were imprisoned and guarded under the law until faith would be revealed. Therefore the law was our disciplinarian until Christ came, so that we might be justified by faith. But now that faith has come, we are no longer subject to a disciplinarian, for in Christ Jesus you are all children of God through faith. As many of you as were baptized into Christ have clothed yourselves with Christ. There is no longer Jew or Greek, there is no longer slave or free, there is no longer male and female; for all of you are one in Christ Jesus. And if you belong to Christ, then you are Abraham's offspring, heirs according to the promise.

Could Jesus have been gay? It almost seems blasphemous to most of us even to ask the question. Something seems to rise up within us screaming an almost vicious *no*. But is not this reaction more an indication of our prejudice against gays than of our reverence for the Lord?

By now most Christians are used to the idea that Jesus was a Jew, though only a couple of generations ago this was difficult for some. I was, sad to say, brought up in a family where there was a lot of prejudice against Jews. I can remember even my saintly mother, who certainly loved our Lord very much and was a woman of prayer, saying some awful things. If I had confronted her with the Jewishness of Jesus, I am sure she would have quickly in her own way made some distinction: "Oh, the Jews in his time were different," or "But he became a Christian."

Whether against gays or Jews or Muslims or welfare recipients or what-have-you, we all have our prejudices. As a tall man, I have to confess my prejudice in favor of height. But if I honestly look around this world, I have to admit that God seems to have a prejudice in favor of the shorter. A white man may feel superior to persons of color, but aren't Caucasians terribly cerebral, cold, lacking in warmth and emotion? So might my Hispanic brother say.

Our Master cuts through all this nonsense (and it is literally non-sense, without sense). His one command, his new commandment: Love one another, love your neighbor as yourself. He makes no distinctions. And to bring the point home to us, he puts two sworn enemies together in one of his most beloved parables: Jew and Samaritan. He certainly would have no difficulty putting gay and straight together, black and white, Jew and Gentile, rich and poor, tall and short, old and young.

Yes, Christ's call and command is all embracing: We are to love everyone with a self-giving love. It is a great challenge for us. We may not be able simply to set aside our deeply engrained prejudices. But we can cut through them. We can reach out. We can, like the Samaritan, take the trouble to be there for the other in spite of the history and the feeling. With the help of God's grace, we can do it.

24 | *Not Far—But Not There Yet*

MARK 12:28–34

One of the scribes came near and heard them disputing . . . and seeing that Jesus answered them well, he asked Jesus, "Which commandment is the first of all?" Jesus answered, "The first is, 'Hear, O Israel: the Lord our God, the Lord is one; you shall love the Lord your God with all your heart, and with all your soul, and with all your mind, and with all your strength.' The second is this, 'You shall love your neighbor as yourself.' There is no other commandment greater than these." Then the scribe said to him, "You are right, Teacher; you have truly said that 'he is one, and besides him there is no other'; and 'to love him with all the heart, and with all the understanding, and with all the strength,' and 'to love one's neighbor as oneself,'—this is much more important than all whole burnt offerings and sacrifices." When Jesus saw that he answered wisely, he said to him, "You are not far from the kingdom of God." After that no one dared to ask him any question.

The Gospel lets us in on an interesting bit of dialogue.

A bright young fellow puts a question to Jesus: Which is the most important commandment?

Jesus responds, as we would all expect: First, to love the Lord your God with all your heart, soul, mind, and strength. Second, to love your neighbor as yourself.

With the cockiness of the young, the inquirer congratulates the Lord for his excellent answer, which he then rephrases.

It is Jesus' turn, and he benignly approves what the lad has had to say, adding: "You are not far from the kingdom of God."

"Not far"—but not quite there, either. For the bright young man's response was that which, in fact, most of us men—and I daresay some women also—give to the Lord's supreme command of love. Yes, love the Lord and neighbor "with all the heart" (in the Scriptures, the heart is the source of willpower), and "with all the understanding" (how we love to escape into the rational thing), and "with all the strength" (yes, our love should be proved in the doing).

But what has our typical male left out?

Jesus named four things. What about the soul—the feelings, the emotions, the source of tenderness and caring?

Alas, we have bought too much into the imaging of our culture, that macho image that we have been trying to export to the rest of the world (you can see the Marlboro man all over China these days). None of that mushy stuff for us!

Are we indeed lacking in soul? Are we afraid of it? Who is actually our model: Jesus or the Marlboro man or Schwarzenegar, or the Terminator, or another of that ilk? Maybe it is time we took a look. Didn't our Master, who was man enough to go unflinching to the cross, say to us: "Learn from me; for I am gentle and humble in heart" (Matthew 11:29)? Wasn't he a tender friend who could let one disciple rest his head upon his bosom, and accept a kiss from another? Yes, the customs of the times, of course, but bespeaking a tender, caring presence.

We haven't arrived at fulfilling the most important commandment, if we have not cultivated a tender, caring love for the Lord Jesus, for it is precisely in him that we find our God. Nor have we fulfilled it if we do not cultivate the same tender, caring love for our neighbors—our friends, our brothers and sisters, our colleagues, our companions on the journey toward the reign of God in our lives and in our world.

How far are we from the kingdom of God?

25 | *Four Comings*

From the fig tree learn its lesson: as soon as its branch becomes tender and puts forth its leaves, you know that summer is near. So also, when you see all these things, you know that he is near, at the very gates. Truly I tell you, this generation will not pass away until all these things have taken place. Heaven and earth will pass away, but my words will not pass away.

But about that day and hour no one knows, neither the angels of heaven, nor the Son, but only the Father. For as the days of Noah were, so will be the coming of the Son of Man. For as in those days before the flood they were eating and drinking, marrying and giving in marriage, until the day Noah entered the ark, and they knew nothing until the flood came and swept them all away, so too will be the coming of the Son of Man. Then two will be in the field; one will be taken and one will be left. Two women will be grinding meal together; one will be taken and one will be left. Keep awake therefore, for you do not know on what day your Lord is coming. But understand this: if the owner of the house had known in what part of the night the thief was coming, he would have stayed awake and would not have let his house be broken into. Therefore you also must be ready, for the Son of Man is coming at an unexpected hour.

During the season of Advent it is undoubtedly the *first* coming of the Lord, the poignant scene of Bethlehem, that most fills our thoughts and imagination: the angels and shepherds, the humble manger, and the lovely couple that gently nurtures the Newborn. Rightly, we celebrate the anniversary of this coming with love, joy, and gratitude. He was born for us, he comes for us. He is our hope and salvation.

But the Lord himself, again and again in the Gospels, speaks rather of his *second* coming. Then he will come in all his glory and might, to bring to completion what he began in Bethlehem. He will take us into his kingdom to share fully in his joy and glory. It was for this that he came. Indeed, it was for this that he created the world: to share his joy, his love, his life.

Probably, most of us will not still be here when that blessed day comes. So we look to a *third* coming: the day he will come in his love to bring each one of us home. Whether that day comes upon us suddenly, like a thief in the night, or comes only after much waiting and longing, he *will* come to take us to the place he has prepared for us.

Most immediately important for each of us is a *fourth* coming: our Lord's constant coming in grace and sacramental mystery. These comings make the difference in our lives. We want always to be expectant, as our Lord tells us. We want to be open and ready for each day's grace.

Christ comes to us to the extent that we want him. It is never God who places the limits. It is we. "Ask, and it will be given you; search, and you will find; knock, and the door will be opened for you. For everyone who asks receives, and everyone who searches finds, and for everyone who knocks, the door will be opened" (Matthew

7:7–8). This is the whole meaning of Advent. It is a time of growth in longing, preparing ourselves for the great graces of Christmas.

When I was a boy, we had different little practices that made Advent real in our lives. It was said that there were four thousand years between the promise of the Redeemer and his coming. And so during the four weeks of Advent we sought to pray four thousand times: "O divine Babe of Bethlehem, whom the angels love and adore, come and take birth in our hearts." Of course, we often lost count and had to devise ways of keeping track of our task. But every day was filled with that prayer of longing.

Then we had the Advent House with its many doors. Each day, together as a family, we opened a door and learned what little practice we were to carry out in preparation for the coming of the Savior.

The good sisters taught us how to prepare the stable of our hearts for the coming of the Newborn. We were to practice so many acts of self-denial during Advent to clean out the stable; so many rosaries to prepare a beautiful seat for Mary; so many Our Fathers to prepare Joseph's place. Then we were to offer so many Masses to prepare the Holy Child's crib: Holy Communions would provide it with silken sheets and comforter.

These Advent tasks, childish though they may seem, kept the holy season very present in our lives and increased our longing for the coming. Today an Advent wreath stands in the center of our home. After the first week the solitary candle is joined by another, and then another—each new candle increasing our longing as it expresses our hope and expectation. We are a sacramental people, and outward signs nourish inner reality.

This is the whole meaning of Advent: to truly seek God. We do this by entering into the liturgy, the life and prayer of the church; and also by weaving our Advent longings into our home life in whatever significant way we can. Living the Lord's fourth coming to the full, we can best honor the first, prepare for the third and be worthy to partake most fully in the second.

Come, Lord Jesus, come!

26 | *You Did It to Me*

MATTHEW 25:31–46

*When the Son of Man comes in his glory, and all
the angels with him, then he will sit on the throne
of his glory. All the nations will be gathered before
him, and he will separate people one from another
as a shepherd separates the sheep from the goats,
and he will put the sheep at his right hand and the
goats at the left. Then the king will say to those
at his right hand, "Come, you that are blessed by
my Father, inherit the kingdom prepared for you
from the foundation of the world; for I was hungry
and you gave me food, I was thirsty and you gave
me something to drink, I was a stranger and you
welcomed me, I was naked and you gave me clothing,
I was sick and you took care of me, I was in prison
and you visited me." Then the righteous will answer
him, "Lord, when was it that we saw you hungry and
gave you food, or thirsty and gave you something to
drink? And when was it that we saw you a stranger
and welcomed you, or naked and gave you clothing?
And when was it that we saw you sick or in prison
and visited you?" And the king will answer them,
"Truly I tell you, just as you did it to one of the least
of these who are members of my family, you did it to
me." Then he will say to those at his left hand, "You
that are accursed, depart from me into the eternal fire
prepared for the devil and his angels; for I was hungry
and you gave me no food, I was thirsty and you gave
me nothing to drink, I was a stranger and you did*

not welcome me, naked and you did not give me clothing, sick and in prison and you did not visit me." Then they also will answer, "Lord, when was it that we saw you hungry or thirsty or a stranger or naked or sick or in prison, and did not take care of you?" Then he will answer them, "Truly I tell you, just as you did not do it to one of the least of these, you did not do it to me." And these will go away into eternal punishment, but the righteous into eternal life.

St. Benedict of Nursia ends his Rule by asking: "What page, what word of the new and old Testaments is not the truest of guides for human life?" If this is true of every word of life that our Lord Jesus has given us, it is certainly true of these five words: "You did it to me."

Back in the seventies, there was a popular musical on Broadway called *Godspell.* With a certain amount of humor, the play enacted the Gospel of St. Matthew. As this particular scene is played out and Jesus speaks the painful words of condemnation, one of the condemned "goats" pops up and says: Lord, if I had known it was you I would have taken you around the corner and bought you a cup of coffee.

A big *if.*

Hearing Jesus' words here, we have little excuse. He makes himself very clear, drawing out his teaching with a striking portrayal. True, it would have had even more impact on his agrarian audience than on urban Americans today. But still we have no difficulty imagining the scene.

If we took to heart the final words of Jesus as he pronounced his judgment, how different would not our whole life be? "You did it to me." If we realized and were constantly conscious that whatever we do to each other, to any human person, we do to Jesus, to the Son of God, to our beloved Savior, how then would we act?

If we realized we are talking to Jesus—even when we are talking to our children, to somebody who is rude to us, to someone who has hurt us, to a subordinate, to the vendor on the corner, to the panhandler—would we say some of the things we say? Or would we speak otherwise?

If we realized that Jesus is in need of clothing, would we leave all those unused or rarely used clothes hanging in our closets? If we knew he is sick, would we put off visiting a sick acquaintance in the hospital? If we knew he is everyone who needs help, would we not perhaps consider giving some of our spare time to prison ministry or to visiting a children's hospital to hold and comfort a little one who desperately needs more human touch? Would we be more generous in stocking the parish food pantry, find time to lend a hand at the soup kitchen?

If we really realized the impact of these words, "You did it to me," would we not consider it a privilege to serve the poor and needy in whatever way we can? If we really loved our Lord, would we not be eager to have this chance to care for him? It is this realization that drove Mother Teresa of Calcutta, who clearly saw Jesus in each person no matter how wretched the least one was.

Stop for a moment. One after the other, let come before your mind's eye the face of each person who is an intimate part of your life. As you see each one, let his or her image fade into the face of Christ. It is the Lord. Then let there come to your mind's eye the face of some of those you have encountered of late: the woman at the checkout counter and the lad doing the bagging, the beggar on the street with his pleading eyes, the person who banged into you as you were trying to leave the elevator or subway. And let each become the Lord. Did we interact with them the way we would really want to, knowing that in responding to them we are responding to our Lord?

"You did it to me." These five little words can be a true guide for our lives. Living them can transform us. Someday Jesus will say to you and to me: "You did it to me." How will we feel then? Which side will we be on at that moment? Will we lamely say: "Lord, if I had known . . . ?"

Passion and Resurrection

27 | *Following in Wonder*

MARK 10:32–34

They were on the road, going up to Jerusalem, and Jesus was walking ahead of them; they were amazed, and those who followed were afraid. He took the twelve aside again and began to tell them what was to happen to him, saying, "See, we are going up to Jerusalem, and the Son of Man will be handed over to the chief priests and the scribes, and they will condemn him to death; then they will hand him over to the Gentiles; they will mock him, and spit upon him, and flog him, and kill him; and after three days he will rise again."

The first instinctive reaction of many of us— maybe men more than women, though I hesitate to generalize in any way—is "I'm no follower!" I may not be a leader, but at least I am not a follower. I'm an independent. I know my own mind, and that is what I follow.

Basically, this is not a bad attitude, if it does not come out of arrogance or pride. We humans are made in the very image of God, and one of our greatest endowments is our freedom. Our Creator made us with innate dignity and allows us freely to determine our course.

But there is a time and place for us freely and with great dignity to choose to be a follower. We can choose to be followers of Jesus Christ, the Son of God, our Savior and our Friend, and this is our greatest glory. I am a follower of Jesus.

In his Gospel, considered by scholars to be the earliest written account of Jesus' life and sayings, Mark opens his account of Jesus' final journey to Jerusalem with words that could be translated: "The disciples were on the road going up to Jerusalem with Jesus walking in the lead. Their mood was one of wonder, while that of those who followed was fear."

What is my mood as I follow Jesus to Jerusalem—the heavenly Jerusalem—wonder or fear? Am I one who follows Jesus according to the fullness of my dignity as a human person? Or am I one who is driven by fear?

Perhaps we do not hear enough today about the fear of hell. Or perhaps we have heard too much about it in the past, more than enough for a lifetime, and therefore no longer take it seriously. There is a legitimate and proper and due fear of the consequences of our own actions. A person who engages in unprotected sex with a stranger should indeed fear the consequences. A person who smokes a pack a day for twenty years should be afraid of the diseases that might result.

And we should always be fearful when we choose to act in defiance of God's will, lest we find ourselves alienated from God forever. For we have no true lasting happiness except in God, in accordance with the wondrous plan he has created for us. In full awareness of God's immense goodness in creating us to enjoy the fullness of his divine happiness forever, certainly another kind of fear also has its due place in our lives—fear of offending such a good Lord, of proving ourselves unworthy and ungrateful.

So there is a place for fear in following our beloved Lord. But a Christian need not suffer from generalized fearfulness, from needless anxiety. For as Jesus said, he is with us at all times, even unto the end of the world. Again and again he says to us: "Fear not." Following him we know, as Paul said, "that all things work together for good for those who love God, who are called according to his purpose" (Romans 8:28).

The choice is ours. God respects the freedom he has given us. We can follow him in fear, but that is not the way his closest friends follow him. They follow him in wonder. Following our Lord, we have no idea of the wondrous joy he has prepared for each one of us in his eternal kingdom. He made us for happiness, for friendship, for fulfillment. I think for many of us it is difficult to grasp such goodness, such love, such wholly gratuitous generosity. But that is our God!

Am I denying the sorrows, pains, and suffering of this life, of the journey? By no means. I know them in my own life. Part of the apostles' wonder comes from what Jesus reveals to them on this journey: that he will suffer wretchedly, be betrayed abysmally, and die miserably, but on the third day he will rise. For those of us who, in the fullness of our human dignity and freedom, choose to follow Jesus, and follow him in wonder, part of our wonder comes from this mystery, the mystery of the cross—how all the suffering and pain of this life in the end, as in the birth of a child, gives way to a joyous outpouring of love in a new life.

The choice is ours: to follow or not to follow, to follow in fear or to follow in wonder. For my part, I have found a joy beyond telling in following Jesus in wonder these past fifty years.

28 | *Why We Observe Lent*

2 TIMOTHY 2:3–14

Share in suffering like a good soldier of Christ Jesus. No one serving in the army gets entangled in every-day affairs; the soldier's aim is to please the enlisting officer. And in the case of an athlete, no one is crowned without competing according to the rules. It is the farmer who does the work who ought to have the first share of the crops. Think over what I say, for the Lord will give you understanding in all things.

Remember Jesus Christ, raised from the dead, a descendant of David—that is my gospel, for which I suffer hardship, even to the point of being chained like a criminal. But the word of God is not chained. Therefore I endure everything for the sake of the elect, so that they may also obtain the salvation that is in Christ Jesus, with eternal glory. The saying is sure:

If we have died with him, we will also live with him;
if we endure, we will also reign with him;
if we deny him, he will also deny us;
if we are faithless, he remains faithful—
for he cannot deny himself.
Remind them of this, and warn them before God that they are to avoid wrangling over words, which does no good but only ruins those who are listening.

For some, Lent is a matter of giving things up. "I am going to give up ice cream for Lent. And candy. And TV."

For others, it is a question of doing things: "I am going to go to weekday Mass." "I am going to skip lunch on Fridays and send the money (and a bit more) to Food for the Poor." "I am going to pray the rosary daily."

These are all good practices. But whether we are giving something up or doing something extra, the important thing is to keep in mind why we are doing what we are doing.

In the beginning of the sixth century St. Benedict of Nursia, one of the great spiritual masters of all times, wrote a Rule that remains the Rule by which most Western monks and nuns live. More than that, today many laypersons are drawing guidance from his Rule as they seek to enrich their lives as Christians and follow Christ more closely. For Benedict, "Nothing is to be preferred to the love of Christ."

In his chapter "On the Observance of Lent," he recommends that we undertake some particular practices during the holy season: "We will add to the usual measure of our service something by way of private prayer and abstinence from food or drink, so that each of us will have something above the assigned measure to offer God of his [or her] own will."

And then St. Benedict adds these words to his admonition: " . . . with joy of the Holy Spirit."

As a later saint observed, a sad saint is a sorry saint. Lent is not to be a time of gloom and sadness, but a time of anticipation and joy—a joy that comes from deep within us, from the Spirit; a joy that is of faith and filled with hope. As Benedict goes on to say: "In other words, let each one deny him [her]self some food, drink, sleep, needless talking and idle jesting, and look forward to holy Easter with joy and spiritual longing."

Joy is the real meaning of our particular Lenten observances, whether they be adding or subtracting. The observances in themselves are not important. In fact, Benedict knows the danger of our making too much of them, so he asks us to make them known to our spiritual father or mother. In the telling of it, we are usually made acutely aware of how little we are undertaking.

The importance of our practices does not lie in the practices themselves, but rather in their helping us to remain at a higher level of consciousness—a Christian consciousness. This consciousness is keenly aware of the paschal mystery that we celebrate in holy Easter: that Christ has died and Christ has risen. And that we shall rise with him and in him—but only if we enter into his passion and death, each in our own way in our own lives.

We "look forward to holy Easter with joy and spiritual longing," because Easter is the ultimate meaning of our lives. What does it profit us if we gain the whole world and suffer the loss of our own very self? The mad scramble for this and that, all the things the media try to convince us consumers we must consume for happiness, may fully fill our time, but it will never fill us. Easter is a celebration of what is truly important and fundamental in our lives—so important that the Christian community since the earliest times has set aside forty days to prepare for its celebration.

This is what Lent is all about: a time of really getting in touch with where our true happiness and fulfillment lies, and abiding more fully in that realization. The daily little practice that we undertake as part of our Lenten observance is a reminder. It calls us back to mindfulness in the midst of a world that is strongly set on distracting us from true values and meaning. So the practice in itself is not important, but we want it to make itself present in our daily lives, challenging us to reflect, to let go of some of the mad rush, to be present to ourselves, to listen to our hearts. What do we really want, deep down? Not what the media or our peers say we should want. What do *we* really want, and where is it to be found?

Ultimately we all want life—unending life, and happiness—complete happiness, in that life. We will find this only in and through the paschal mystery, through our entering into the passion, death, and resurrection of Christ. We all know this in faith. But all too often our faith is like the good seed that fell among the thorns. It gets choked up by the cares and concerns of our journey through this world. Lent is a time to cut back those thorns a bit, to let some things go, to introduce something that will help us grow, be it manure or the divine light that comes from prayer, Scripture, and meditation.

Benedict urges each to choose a special book for Lent, and to read it clear through. This may well mean cutting back on TV, magazines, or newspapers. A little less of them each day to make room for a little more of the Lord's word. This indeed can be a source of nourishing light.

What am I going to do for Lent? Yes, I will give up peanut butter. (I love it!) But I will also spend at least a half hour each day with the Scriptures, listening to the Lord, letting him lead me more deeply into the paschal mystery. And I shall look forward eagerly to celebrating that Mystery and entering into it more fully than ever before.

29 | *The Power of the Blood*

MATTHEW 26:17–30

On the first day of Unleavened Bread the disciples came to Jesus, saying, "Where do you want us to make the preparations for you to eat the Passover?" He said, "Go into the city to a certain man, and say to him, 'The Teacher says, My time is near; I will keep the Passover at your house with my disciples.'" So the disciples did as Jesus had directed them, and they prepared the Passover meal.

When it was evening, he took his place with the twelve; and while they were eating, he said, "Truly I tell you, one of you will betray me." And they became greatly distressed and began to say to him one after another, "Surely not I, Lord?" He answered, "The one who has dipped his hand into the bowl with me will betray me. The Son of Man goes as it is written of him, but woe to that one by whom the Son of Man is betrayed! It would have been better for that one not to have been born." Judas, who betrayed him, said, "Surely not I, Rabbi?" He replied, "You have said so."

While they were eating, Jesus took . . . bread, and after blessing it he broke it, gave it to the disciples, and said, "Take, eat; this is my body." Then he took a cup, and after giving thanks he gave it to them, saying, "Drink from it, all of you; for this is my blood of the covenant, which is poured out for many for the forgiveness of sins. I tell you, I will never again drink of this fruit of the vine until that day

when I drink it new with you in my Father's kingdom."
When they had sung the hymn, they went out to the
Mount of Olives.

The Passover is one of the most exciting stories of salvation history. It may be myth, that vehicle that bears truth too big for mere conceptual prose but rather resorts to the richness of poetry and tale. It tells us of the saving power of our God.

Moses, instructed by God, tells all the Hebrew people to gather in their homes. Each household is to slaughter a lamb, a perfect lamb, a lamb without blemish. Then the blood of the lamb is to be sprinkled on the doorposts of the house. All are to stay within, enjoy a feast of roast lamb, and get ready for a speedy departure. During the night the angel of the Lord swoops down on a terrible mission, finally to win the listening of a people and a ruler who ever closed their ears to the message of the Lord. The angel is to slay the firstborn son of each household. But wherever the angel sees the blood sprinkled upon the doorposts, the angel is to pass by.

Was it the blood of a dumb animal that saved the lives of rational animals, asks St. John Chrysostom? No! Rather, what did the angel see? The angel saw, not the blood of a lamb, but the blood of the Lamb of God. What was done in sacramental symbol that night in the Egypt of bondage is done in reality in the world where sin holds us all in bondage. It is the blood of the Lamb—the Lamb who is God's own Son—on our lips, the doorposts of the temple that we are, that saves us from the onslaughts of the angel who would now wreak havoc, the fallen angel, the evil spirit we call the devil or Satan.

This is the power of the blood. We drink the cup of salvation, the precious blood of the Lord, which poured forth from his side when he slept the sleep of death upon the cross, but which he had already given us in sacramental mystery the night before in the cup of the new covenant. Signed with this saving blood, we are safe.

The saving power of the blood will be sacramentally prefigured as Moses leads the redeemed people out through the Red Sea, our baptism; through the desert, our pilgrim journey through life; into the land of promise, the kingdom which has been promised to us. It is because we have been saved by the blood of the Lamb that we belong to the people of God and, led by our God-anointed leader, can confidently go forward knowing that the kingdom is our promised heritage.

Easter is a special time. The blood is fresh upon our lips. We go forward with the joy and enthusiasm of a new beginning, a vibrant hope. We vaguely know that the dog days of summer are ahead when we will have to plod along faithfully, struggling to keep our hope green. But for now, the risen Lord is very much with us. He has not yet ascended, going ahead to prepare the place for us. He walks at our side, opens the Scriptures for us, feeds us, challenges us, encourages us, prepares us for all that is to come. It is a good time. We know a oneness with him, for we have been bonded in his blood. We are more than blood brothers and sisters. We have all received his Spirit, and all together we cry out, with full confidence and love: Abba, Our Father.

This is the power of the blood. This is the joy of Easter.

30 | *At the Last Supper*

Ask and Receive

JOHN 16:21–27

When a woman is in labor, she has pain, because her hour has come. But when her child is born, she no longer remembers the anguish because of the joy of having brought a human being into the world. So you have pain now; but I will see you again, and your hearts will rejoice, and no one will take your joy from you. On that day you will ask nothing of me. Very truly, I tell you, if you ask anything of the Father in my name, he will give it to you. Until now you have not asked for anything in my name. Ask and you will receive, so that your joy may be complete.

I have said these things to you in figures of speech. The hour is coming when I will no longer speak to you in figures, but will tell you plainly of the Father. On that day you will ask in my name. I do not say to you that I will ask the Father on your behalf; for the Father himself loves you, because you have loved me and have believed that I came from God.

You have probably heard it, as have I: God never hears my prayers; he never answers—if there is a God. He said: "Ask and you will receive." But I ask and ask and never get anything.

I might answer with our Lord's little story of the pesky widow and the unjust judge (you can read the story in Luke 18:1–8). We do have to be persistent in our praying. But even then . . .

I think when we come to prayer we are sometimes like little children sitting on Santa's knee. We expect the benign Father to give us whatever we ask. We need to be childlike, but not childish. That is an important distinction. We see the shiny carving knife and want the immediate gratification of playing with it, in no way imagining what life without a finger or a hand might be like.

It might be better to see ourselves as mature children sitting down with our Father to look at things together and see what is best. Or, mindful of our Lord Jesus' words, "I have called you friends" (John 15:15), we might see ourselves as sitting with the Son, our friend. Before we ask for something, we need to take the time to see what we most want, and we need to consider whether the thing that looks gratifying to us at the moment is really conducive to that. As our wiser, more provident Father may see, what we are asking for now may, like the carving knife, lead to a real truncation, not only for a lifetime but for eternity.

Yes, ask and you will receive. But often it is not what we say we want but what we really want that God gives us: that which is conducive to our true and lasting happiness. Life on earth is immensely important. Every moment is precious and not to be squandered. But as important as our present life is, eternal life is infinitely more precious. God answers in the context of eternity.

God may seem to be saying no. He may even appear to turn a deaf ear. But in fact no prayer goes unheard or unanswered. We can take that on faith. And someone wiser than we is answering out of God's infinite wisdom.

On the night before he died, Jesus had a very special farewell meal with his chosen friends. In the course of that meal, the disciple who loved Jesus sat next to him, or rather in the fashion of that time, reclined next to Jesus so that he could lean back and rest his head on Jesus' chest and hear the beating of Jesus' heart. He hung onto every word Jesus spoke on that fateful night. And in later years, with the help of Holy Spirit, he shared Jesus' words again and again until they were finally written down.

Among the words recorded are these: "I have said these things to you so that my joy may be in you, and that your joy may be complete" (John 15:11). All is to our joy—if we do it God's way.

And so, instinctively, while we ask for various things, we often add the proviso, as Jesus did in Gethsemane: ". . . yet, not my will but yours be done" (Luke 22:42). Father, do whatever you know is best for us. It seems to me that this is best for me right now, but you know. Your will be done—on earth as in heaven.

Ask and you will receive—whatever is for your true happiness and well-being, whether for yourself or for others. For the same infinite wisdom holds each of our dear ones, for each of whom we pray, in tender and caring love.

31 | *At the Last Supper*

Made for Joy

JOHN 17:6–13 NAB

I revealed your name to those whom you gave me out of the world. They belonged to you, and you gave them to me, and they have kept your word. Now they know that everything you gave me is from you, because the words you gave to me I have given to them, and they accepted them and truly understood that I came from you, and they have believed that you sent me. I pray for them. I do not pray for the world but for the ones you have given me, because they are yours, and everything of mine is yours and everything of yours is mine, and I have been glorified in them. And now I will no longer be in the world, but they are in the world, while I am coming to you. Holy Father, keep them in your name that you have given me, so that they may be one just as we are. When I was with them I protected them in your name that you gave me, and I guarded them, and none of them was lost except the son of destruction, in order that the scripture might be fulfilled. But now I am coming to you. I speak this in the world so that they may share my joy completely.

Why did God make you? A fundamental question!

I can hear the old catechism answer buzzing around: God made me to know, love, and serve him in this world and to be happy with him in the next. That answer has probably driven more people out of the church than anything else. A god who wants us to *serve* him here and be happy with him only *someday* out there. Pie in the sky! That's not our God!

God the Father and God the Son and God Holy Spirit were completely happy, enjoying each other to the full. Well, what do you want to do when you are very happy? You want to share your happiness. God looked around, and there was no one with whom to share happiness. So that's why God made you and me—to share God's happiness, not just someday off in the sky, but right here and now.

At the Last Supper, after opening his heart to us—"I do not call you servants any longer, because the servant does not know what the master is doing; but I have called you friends, because I have made known to you everything that I have heard from my Father" (John 15:15)—Jesus said to his Father: "I speak this in the world so that they may share my joy completely."

St. Gregory Nazianzen, whom our Byzantine brothers and sisters call St. Gregory the Theologian, was archbishop of Constantinople. Exhorting his people to gratitude and generosity, he said: "Acknowledge whence you have existence, breath, and understanding. Acknowledge whence you have what is most important of all, your knowledge of God, your hope of the kingdom of heaven, your contemplation of glory which in this life is of course through a glass darkly but hereafter will be more perfect and clearer. Acknowledge that you have been made a child of God, co-heir with Christ. Acknowledge, and now I speak with daring, that you have been made divine" (taken from a reading from the addresses of St. Gregory

Nazianzen, prepared by the Pontifical University St. Thomas Aquinas).

What Gregory says "with daring" is true: We have been made divine. It had to be that way, for God made us to share his happiness—fully. Many of us have a dog or a cat, and it is a great friend. But when we have a deep human joy to share, we don't usually go to our dog or cat. We seek out a friend who can truly enter into our human joy.

Likewise we had to be made in some way divine so that we could truly share the joy of the Lord. That is what happened at baptism, we have been baptized into Christ, made one with him in a oneness beyond anything we can imagine. We have become one with the Son of God. And that is part of what we prepare during Lent to celebrate at Easter: our divinization, our participation in divine life, the gateway to divine happiness for each one of us.

32 | *At the Last Supper*

God Within Us

JOHN 14:23–27

Jesus answered him, "Those who love me will keep my word, and my Father will love them, and we will come to them and make our home with them. Whoever does not love me does not keep my words; and the word that you hear is not mine, but is from the Father who sent me. I have said these things to you while I am still with you. But the Advocate, the Holy Spirit, whom the Father will send in my name, will teach you everything, and remind you of all that I have said to you. Peace I leave with you; my peace I give to you. I do not give it to you as the world gives. Do not let your hearts be troubled, and do not let them be afraid."

Yes, the Lord is present within us. We know that by faith. We heard him say it, on the night before he died, when he opened his heart to his chosen friends: "Those who love me will keep my word, and my Father will love them, and we will come to them and make our home with them" (John 14:23).

God is present within us. I am afraid many of us think of this presence as if our heart or some other chamber deep within us were a sort of tabernacle where the Lord is present as he is present in the tabernacle in church, though not quite so real a presence. Just real enough to make us feel guilty that we are not more faithful in paying our due visits to him.

If we have grown a bit in spiritual awareness, we sense a more spiritual presence, less tied to a specific place. God is a distinct Person with whom I relate. God is everywhere, and I happen to be one of the places where God is. So are others: Whatever you do to my least ones, you do to me. Hence reverence is due every human person—including myself.

But God's presence is even more personal than that. More profoundly and intimately, God, in the reality of being the divine creative energy, is present in us. We tend to think of creation as if God made something, tossed it out there, and let it go on by itself. That is far from the reality. With God there is no past or future. God is *now*. Now, and at every moment, God is creating us—bringing us forth in a constant creative act of his divine love.

All that I am and all that I do is of God's creative energy. And God is not distinct from his creative energy. God *is* his creative energy. It is only by his creative energy that I do anything at all. God in me, through me, with me, is typing these keys. If I lift my hand, it is by the divine creative energy, here and now, operating in and with me: "Apart from me you can do nothing" (John 15:5). We have heard this word of his, but to what extent do we understand it and effectively believe that it applies to our daily lives?

This is an awesome reality. God puts himself at our disposal. We can use the divine creative energy in any way we want, for good or for something less than good. This is the humility of our God, the self-giving love of our God—a prodigal Father who entrusts his very self to his children.

We know we are made in the image of God. This image is more than a painting, an icon, an external like-ness. It is even more than a son or daughter: "She is the image of her mother." We do not have an adequate word to express this unique relationship. We are in real-ity a presence of the divine creative energy. This energy acts in, through, and with us. It is brought to divine lev-els when we allow divine grace to operate freely within us: "God has sent the Spirit of his Son into our hearts, crying, 'Abba! Father!'" (Galatians 4:6).

Holy Spirit becomes one with our spirit in a unity that defies our ability to express it, just as we cannot give adequate expression to the unity of the Father, Son, and Holy Spirit, a unity that makes Three absolutely One. Yes, this oneness with the divine creative energy makes us one, not only with God, but with everyone else who is one with God; that is, in varying degrees, with all creation (hence the demand for a true ecology), but in a very special way with every human person.

Short of pantheism, how can we exaggerate the sublimity of who we actually are, of the potential and the responsibility of what we do? How can we thank the Lord sufficiently for who he has made us? With the Psalmist, we cry: "I praise you, for I am fearfully and wonderfully made" (Psalm 139:14).

33 | *The Wounded Heart*

ISAIAH 53:1–6 NAB

Who would believe what we have heard?
To whom has the arm of the Lord been revealed?
He grew up like a sapling before him,
like a shoot from the parched earth;
There was in him no stately bearing to make us look at him,
nor appearance that would attract us to him.
He was spurned and avoided by men,
a man of suffering, accustomed to infirmity,
One of those from whom men hide their faces,
spurned, and we held him in no esteem.

Yet it was our infirmities that he bore,
our sufferings that he endured,
While we thought of him as stricken,
as one smitten by God and afflicted.
But he was pierced for our offenses,
crushed for our sins,
Upon him was the chastisement that makes us whole,
by his stripes we were healed.
We had all gone astray like sheep,
each following his own way;
But the Lord laid upon him
the guilt of us all.

The pierced heart of Christ is the ultimate symbol of his burning love for us. When he had given everything else, finally the soldier pierced his heart. It could no longer beat, but it poured forth water and blood, symbols of its ongoing love, which we would experience in baptism and in the Eucharist, the chalice of life.

The wounded heart of Christ speaks to us of more than his great, totally self-giving love. It also speaks to us of the sufferings of all our sisters and brothers within whom he even now suffers. Every age including our own has known those who, like their and our Lord, have given their all. Ours is a new age of martyrs: our four sisters in Central America, the Jesuits and their devoted housekeeper, our beloved archbishop Romero, our own Cistercian brothers who were beheaded in Algiers, seven of the multitude of priests and religious who have died for the faith in that country. And all the less known: in East Timor and north India, the hundreds being crucified (literally) in Sudan, those dying in the prisons of China, and so many more.

The heart of Christ is wounded not only in our martyrs. It is wounded also in the multitudes who suffer and die daily because of the horrors of economic oppression. Most of us in the United States have known an abundant life. We have food, shelter, medical care, and so much more. How tragically different it is just south of our border in countries like Haiti and Mexico.

Indeed, we do not need even to step outside this land of abundance to find human suffering. In how many of our cities, and also in the hills and other depressed areas, are there sisters and brothers without habitation worthy of humans, without regular meals with sufficient nourishment for basic health, without the clothing they need to face the rigors of climate?

This wounding is all the more tragic because it exists in intimate contact with vast fortunes, with people who receive salaries thousands of times above the poverty level and yet expend no effort to use their accumulating wealth to save the life and human dignity of Christ in these least ones. They are too busy. They have time only for their efforts to increase their own wealth and power.

Yet Jesus, the wounded heart, is one with these his least: the hungry, the thirsty, the naked, the homeless, the sick, the imprisoned. Sadly, we spend vast sums to imprison Christ (a billion-dollar industry with advocates of privatization seeking to convert it to individual profit) rather than developing programs that will heal the causes of crime and provide opportunities for reform.

When we look upon the pierced heart of Jesus, we are challenged not only with the reality of his great love which went to such great lengths for us, but by his gaping wounds all about us in his and our sisters and brothers. We hear the words: Look upon him whom you have pierced—for we all have pierced him by our sins—and we know we must do something now, today, to heal his wounds.

Prayers and acts of repentance and reparation to the Sacred Heart are important, but they are not enough. We want to respond to the wounds he is now suffering in those who walk with us now on the earth. We want to do what we can, according to our means, material and spiritual, to bring comfort, healing and well-being. If we do not do this, whatever devotion we seek to bring to the Sacred Heart will be hollow. We cannot minister only to the head. Ours is the joy and privilege to be able to serve and solace the whole Christ.

34 | *Look upon Him*

JOHN 19:18–37

*There they crucified him, and with him two others,
one on either side, with Jesus between them. Pilate
also had an inscription written and put on the cross.
It read, "Jesus of Nazareth, the King of the Jews."
Many of the Jews read this inscription, because the
place where Jesus was crucified was near the city;
and it was written in Hebrew, in Latin, and in Greek.
Then the chief priests of the Jews said to Pilate,
"Do not write, 'The King of the Jews,' but, 'This
man said, I am King of the Jews.'" Pilate answered,
"What I have written I have written." When the soldiers had crucified Jesus, they took his clothes and
divided them into four parts, one for each soldier.
They also took his tunic; now the tunic was seamless,
woven in one piece from the top. So they said to one
another, "Let us not tear it, but cast lots for it to see
who will get it." This was to fulfill what the scripture
says,*

> *"They divided my clothes among themselves,
> and for my clothing they cast lots."*

And that is what the soldiers did.

*Meanwhile, standing near the cross of Jesus were
his mother, and his mother's sister, Mary the wife
of Clopas, and Mary Magdalene. When Jesus saw
his mother and the disciple whom he loved standing
beside her, he said to his mother, "Woman, here is
your son." Then he said to the disciple, "Here is your*

mother." And from that hour the disciple took her into his own home.

After this, when Jesus knew that all was now finished, he said (in order to fulfill the scripture), "I am thirsty." A jar full of sour wine was standing there. So they put a sponge full of the wine on a branch of hyssop and held it to his mouth. When Jesus had received the wine, he said, "It is finished." Then he bowed his head and gave up his spirit.

Since it was the day of Preparation, the Jews did not want the bodies left on the cross during the sabbath, especially because that sabbath was a day of great solemnity. So they asked Pilate to have the legs of the crucified men broken and the bodies removed. Then the soldiers came and broke the legs of the first and of the other who had been crucified with him. But when they came to Jesus and saw that he was already dead, they did not break his legs. Instead, one of the soldiers pierced his side with a spear, and at once blood and water came out. (He who saw this has testified so that you also may believe. His testimony is true, and he knows that he tells the truth.) These things occurred so that the scripture might be fulfilled, "None of his bones shall be broken." And again another passage of scripture says, "They will look on the one whom they have pierced."

The chosen people were on a journey, a long journey through the desert. They had sinned and sinned again, causing their journey to be prolonged. Now their sins brought among them poisonous serpents. The bite of these creatures meant death. The people cried out for healing. And an ever-compassionate God gave Moses the command: Fashion a bronze figure and raise it on a cross. All who look upon it will be healed. (The story is told in Numbers 21:4–9.)

Jesus is raised upon a cross above the city and outside its walls, for he is raised up not only for this city and these people, but for us all. Jesus is raised on high, and many look upon him. Pilate tried to determine what they should see: "The King of the Jews," his inscription read. But others had other eyes.

Some saw a hated rival, a threat to their power, finally being overcome—so they thought—and they mocked and reviled him. Some saw a beloved in agony, and they agonized with him. One thief saw another beaten man and cursed all the more. But another thief saw something more and asked to go along on the journey into paradise. And it was an executioner, a pagan soldier, who cried out: "Truly this man was God's Son!" (Mark 15:39).

What do we see as we look upon him who has been pierced? Do we look with faith and hope and find healing? Do we really believe this is the Son of God, and that in his death is our life? As we struggle with the death-dealing wounds of sin, we need to look upon the one who has been raised up. There is no other salvation for us. He alone can save us from eternal death.

It is not enough for us to stand there with the sinless Virgin and experience something of the horror and pain of what is taking place. We are not sinless. We are deeply wounded by sin. And it is only if we look upon the crucified one, experience the price of our sin, and truly repent, that we can know the healing grace. The more we know the agony and pain our sins have caused and have demanded in their reparation, the more our looking upon this one who has been raised up is apt to be effective in our healing.

We have to be willing to acknowledge and expose our wounds to the healing balm that flows from the pierced hands and feet and side. We need humbly and gratefully to accept this healing, with a gratitude that impels us to seek to sin no more. Then our looking upon him who has been pierced will be for us a saving glance. If we want to abide in our healed state, we need constantly to look upon him. The crucifix should not be just an ornament in our homes. It should be a constant invitation to an ever-deeper communion. He has been pierced for our offenses. In his wounds we are healed. Let us go forward in gratitude and in newness of life.

Perhaps our model here should be "the disciple whom [Jesus] loved." What enabled this young man to stay the course, when all the others had run? What made him worthy to hear: "Here is your mother"? What led him in all his writings to speak of himself as "the disciple whom he loved"?

Was it what he saw in those eyes, obscured though they were with blood, sweat, tears, and spittle? Even on Calvary, as he looked into those eyes, John had that ineffable experience of being the object of another's delight, of being truly accepted, embraced, and loved. Jesus had said: Seek and you will find. John had sought. And he found. He found love.

We, too, if we seek love in the face of the Beloved, will find love. Perhaps it is most easily found in the face of the Crucified. "No one has greater love than this, to lay down one's life for one's friends" (John 15:13). The experience will be ours if only we dare, with openness, to look upon him. To look into those eyes and let the love pour in. It scares us, of course—even though we long for it with our whole being. It scares us, because the only response to such love is love; we will have to give ourselves in return. But it is only in this communion of love that we will find all that we seek, as persons raised up to share divine life, joy, and being.

35 | *He Descended into Hell*

1 PETER 3:18–22

For Christ also suffered for sins once for all, the righteous for the unrighteous, in order to bring you to God. He was put to death in the flesh, but made alive in the spirit, in which also he went and made a proclamation to the spirits in prison, who in former times did not obey, when God waited patiently in the days of Noah, during the building of the ark, in which a few, that is, eight persons, were saved through water. And baptism, which this prefigured, now saves you—not as a removal of dirt from the body, but as an appeal to God for a good conscience, through the resurrection of Jesus Christ, who has gone into heaven and is at the right hand of God, with angels, authorities, and powers made subject to him.

We are all familiar with the Jonah story, his three days and three nights in the belly of the great fish, as a type or prophetic image of our Lord's time in the tomb before his glorious resurrection. Jesus himself pointed to Jonah's story. But the wondrous experience of three young men in ancient Babylon also speaks to us of our Lord's victory over sin and death.

Three young Hebrews dancing in the flames of a furnace made seven times hotter than usual—it was a favorite picture on the walls of the Roman catacombs and in medieval manuscripts, and it's still popular in children's Bible-story coloring books today. King Nebuchadnezzar had commanded these fine young lads to worship his false god. They would have none of it, even if disobedience cost their lives. Would to God such courage and steadfastness were found among all our young people today in the face of our society's false gods! Rather than give in to phoniness, these young men of old courageously allowed themselves to be bound hand and foot and thrown into the furnace. And soon they were dancing with a fourth—the Son of Man met them in the flames.

In our English translation of the Apostles' Creed we say, rather crudely, "He descended into hell." Concepts were not yet so polished in those early days of Christianity, when this ancient creed was formulated. The distinction had not been clearly made between the realm of eternal damnation, which is what we usually mean by *hell,* and the place where all the just who died before our Lord's redeeming death waited (at least according to our sequence of time) until he opened to them the gates of paradise. Their waiting place was, in a way, hell. They were still under the dominion of the evil one in the realm of the unredeemed. And then the Redeemer went to them, danced with them, and led them forth to accompany him in his ascent into heaven, just as he had come down into Nebuchadnezzar's fiery furnace to dance with the Hebrew boys, and led them out of the flames into honored places in that kingdom.

What is the point of all this for us?

Don't we all, at one time or another, know our own hells? If in those dark or fiery hours, we can but open the eyes of our faith, we will see that then, more than ever, the Son of Man, our Redeemer is with us. And he will lead us forth.

This is the meaning of the resurrection. Yes, it proves beyond any doubt that Jesus is who he says he is. But it is also a clear manifestation of his victory over sin, over all the consequences of sin—which is what all our sufferings are—and over death. His is the victory. And it is also our victory, we who have been baptized into Christ.

If in the midst of all our sufferings, we can, at least for a few minutes, leave the consciousness of them aside and turn within to the place where the Lord dwells, resting with him, we can know that the victory is ours. We will certainly be able to do this more easily in our times of hell, if at other times—indeed, if each day—we take time to go within and rest in the healing presence of our Redeemer.

Easter is every day. But it is especially those days when we are in hell and he descends into hell to be with us, to refresh us even in the flames, to dance with us as he did with the three young men, and to lead us forth in the sure confidence that victory is ours in the risen Christ.

36 | *The Resurrection of the Body*

Now the chief priests and the elders persuaded the crowds to ask for Barabbas and to have Jesus killed. The governor again said to them, "Which of the two do you want me to release for you?" And they said, "Barabbas." Pilate said to them, "Then what should I do with Jesus who is called the Messiah?" All of them said, "Let him be crucified!" Then he asked, "Why, what evil has he done?" But they shouted all the more, "Let him be crucified!"

So when Pilate saw that he could do nothing, but rather that a riot was beginning, he took some water and washed his hands before the crowd, saying, "I am innocent of this man's blood; see to it your- selves." Then the people as a whole answered, "His blood be on us and on our children!" So he released Barabbas for them; and after flogging Jesus, he handed him over to be crucified.

Then the soldiers of the governor took Jesus into the governor's headquarters, and they gathered the whole cohort around him. They stripped him and put a scarlet robe on him, and after twisting some thorns into a crown, they put it on his head. They put a reed in his right hand and knelt before him and mocked him, saying, "Hail, King of the Jews!" They spat on him, and took the reed and struck him on the head. After mocking him, they stripped him of the robe and put his own clothes on him. Then they led him away to crucify him.

As they went out, they came upon a man from Cyrene named Simon; they compelled this man to carry his cross. And when they came to a place called Golgotha (which means Place of a Skull), they offered him wine to drink, mixed with gall; but when he tasted it, he would not drink it. And when they had crucified him, they divided his clothes among themselves by casting lots; then they sat down there and kept watch over him.

The Tenth Station: Jesus is stripped of his garments. We hardly dare to picture it in our mind's eye, certainly not in our tableaux. Here God's descent to participate in our humanity is fully revealed—a man like ourselves in all but sin.

It was Adam's and Eve's shame at their nakedness that betrayed their sin. The beauty of one of God's loveliest creations, the human body, could no longer be appreciated. We now strip in shame or in secret for our secret sins. Can we look upon our naked Lord—for surely he was stripped naked; it was a routine part of this brutal, degrading death—and not cringe?

Jesus' beautiful body has been horribly violated. It is lacerated, bruised, and defiled: caked blood, the dirt of the streets, spittle. It stands, or lies, before us today in bodies emaciated from hunger, battered in domestic violence, brutalized in our prisons, desecrated by sexual harassment, discarded in dumpsters behind abortion clinics. What are we going to do about it? Simply turn our heads in horror and try to forget it? Continue to strip ourselves and others in our lust? Deny our common humanity, which we share even with this degraded God? Is it not time instead to seek out and minister to the stripped Christ in our midst?

"They put him to death by hanging him on a tree; but God raised him on the third day and allowed him to appear" (Acts 10:39–40). Jesus rose on the third day. That precious body, so beaten and battered and finally drained of life, and hastily hidden away in a borrowed tomb, now stands in our midst, truly the most beautiful of the sons of woman. Now the wounds glisten, jewels of rarest beauty, proclaiming a victory beyond imagination. How does the battered Christ of today rise up? Through your ministry and mine.

"I believe in the resurrection of the body," I say when I repeat the Apostles' Creed, but it is an empty proclamation if I do not do what I can to bring about that resurrection—not on the third day but today. The ministries are waiting, indeed, crying out. For prayer—yes! For money—yes! But above all for persons, for caring brothers and sisters who can make a difference.

Let us celebrate the resurrection, once a year and every Sunday, by actually doing something to bring about the resurrection of the body of Christ, which we, the human family, are. "I believe in the resurrection of the body." What am I doing to make it happen?

37 | *New Life*

COLOSSIANS 3:1–4

So if you have been raised with Christ, seek the things that are above, where Christ is, seated at the right hand of God. Set your minds on things that are above, not on things that are on earth, for you have died, and your life is hidden with Christ in God. When Christ who is your life is revealed, then you also will be revealed with him in glory.

All creation is cyclic. Each thing passes and gives place to the new. The seed falls in the ground and dies, and it gives birth to new life. But the forces of nature always engender the same kind of life.

On Easter eve each year, thousands all over the world go down into the water and die with Christ to rise to a new life. Each of us, the baptized, whether we remember it or not, whether we were submerged or poured upon, went down and rose to a new life. This spiritual life is not like the life that went before it. It is wholly different; it wholly transcends the life we lived before baptism.

The purpose of the long and wondrous liturgy of Easter eve is to renew our consciousness. We have died, we have risen, we have a new life. But it is a new life "hidden with Christ in God." It is a reality known only by faith, and the experience flowing from faith.

Faith comes from hearing the word, from experiencing the symbols. All the words and symbols of the great Easter Vigil speak to us of the new life that is ours: the new fire—a spark leaping out of a rock and producing a great blaze; the candle—carrying light wherever it goes, a light that can spread and overcome the darkness; the readings—of the creation coming into being, of a people liberated by passing through the sea, of a promised land filled with divine presence and benevolence.

In that special and most sacred night, as the blessed water is sprinkled on us all, we renew our promises, our vows, our baptism, begging the Lord to renew in us all the grace of that sacrament and bring us to a new and higher consciousness of who we are as men and women baptized into Christ: "It is no longer I who live, but it is Christ who lives in me. And the life I now live in the flesh I live by faith in the Son of God, who loved me and gave himself for me" (Galatians 2:20). I have died—my life is hidden with Christ in God.

If I live according to who I am, I do seek the things that are above, not of the earth. I see everything from a new perspective.

Indeed, I still see the things of this creation, of the earth. But I see them now in a truer light. I see them all as an expression of God's love. I see them all according to their place in God's plan. I appreciate them more and find more joy in them; because I am no longer grabbing at them to find some passing pleasure, but I am letting them be to me in Christ a gift of beauty, life, and love.

The Easter liturgy invites us all to rise to this higher, richer, fuller, and truer level of consciousness. "Seek the things that are above," for "your life is hidden with Christ in God."

Christ is risen. He is truly risen. He has ascended to the Father. And we have been baptized into the risen Christ, who is now hidden from us in God, but known and experienced in the clear light of faith and through these symbols of faith.

Easter is the time when we are invited to renew our faith, to rise to a higher consciousness, to find in everything a greater joy, because we have died to a grasping life and live in Christ Jesus where all things are ours, we are Christ's, and Christ is God's.

38 | *Sharing the Good News*

LUKE 24:13-35

*Now on that same day two of them were going to
a village called Emmaus, about seven miles from
Jerusalem, and talking with each other about all these
things that had happened. While they were talking
and discussing, Jesus himself came near and went
with them, but their eyes were kept from recognizing
him. And he said to them, "What are you discussing
with each other while you walk along?" They stood
still, looking sad. Then one of them, whose name was
Cleopas, answered him, "Are you the only stranger
in Jerusalem who does not know the things that have
taken place there in these days?" He asked them,
"What things?" They replied, "The things about
Jesus of Nazareth, who was a prophet mighty in deed
and word before God and all the people, and how
our chief priests and leaders handed him over to be
condemned to death and crucified him. But we had
hoped that he was the one to redeem Israel. Yes, and
besides all this, it is now the third day since these
things took place. Moreover, some women of our
group astounded us. They were at the tomb early this
morning, and when they did not find his body there,
they came back and told us that they had indeed seen
a vision of angels who said that he was alive. Some
of those who were with us went to the tomb and
found it just as the women had said; but they did not
see him." Then he said to them, "Oh, how foolish
you are, and how slow of heart to believe all that*

the prophets have declared! Was it not necessary that the Messiah should suffer these things and then enter into his glory?" Then beginning with Moses and all the prophets, he interpreted to them the things about himself in all the scriptures.

As they came near the village to which they were going, he walked ahead as if he were going on. But they urged him strongly, saying, "Stay with us, because it is almost evening and the day is now nearly over." So he went in to stay with them. When he was at the table with them, he took bread, blessed and broke it, and gave it to them. Then their eyes were opened, and they recognized him; and he vanished from their sight. They said to each other, "Were not our hearts burning within us while he was talking to us on the road, while he was opening the scriptures to us?" That same hour they got up and returned to Jerusalem; and they found the eleven and their companions gathered together. They were saying, "The Lord has risen indeed, and he has appeared to Simon!" Then they told what had happened on the road, and how he had been made known to them in the breaking of the bread.

Yes, they dashed back to Jerusalem—a day's journey done in hours. They had their good news, only to be greeted by good news. For Simon Peter, too, had his story. And it had become the story of all, and all were eager to relate it.

Have you heard the latest?

We are—most of us—all too eager to share "the latest," whatever tidbit of gossip is making the rounds, often without taking care as to its veracity. We also happily share the latest joke, what happened on the gridiron, the event of the hour. But for some reason, most of us are hesitant to share our faith, what we have heard from the Lord, what spoke to us in Sunday's Gospel or homily.

We certainly do not want to appear preachy or holier than thou. And we certainly do not want to shove the Bible down anyone's throat. But there is a way humbly and lovingly to share what we have received. What is the second great commandment? To love our neighbor as ourselves. What have we received and been enriched by? What has been good for us? Shouldn't we want to share this with our loved ones and friends?

We are all one in Christ. What the Lord gives us, he gives for the sake of us all. More, we are each Christ. Having been baptized into Christ, we can truly be Christ to one another, bringing to one another something of his saving word and its meaning in our lives.

Some structures can help us to do this. A faith-sharing group that gathers just for this purpose is very helpful. Every parish should sponsor such groups. In some areas the base communities are alive and active, sharing in this way. Perhaps the family, before it rises from the supper table on Saturday evening, could together listen to the next day's Gospel and each share what he or she hears.

But there is lots of room for informal sharing. Faith sharing can be just a word in the course of walking along or sharing a ride with a friend. A simple "God bless you" as we part—even at the checkout counter—is faith sharing. It tells the other that we believe there is a God, and that he cares and blesses. I have found that such a word of blessing has almost always evoked a positive response, and sometimes a very enthusiastic one.

With friends and family we can take the initiative: What did you get out of the Gospel today? I wonder what it means for us. What did you think of Father's homily? Wasn't that a good point . . . ? We can inaugurate such sharing even with our young children or grandchildren, listening to what they have heard and adding our own contribution. Our eagerness to hear will encourage them, and we will often be richly rewarded. "Out of the mouths of infants and nursing babies you have prepared praise for yourself" (Matthew 21:16).

You never know: you may share a word with your loved ones or friends that the Lord will use to change and enrich the rest of their lives. What a joy that can be. I have had people say to me: "Boy, when you said . . . , that really hit me. I have never forgotten it." And what they say I said is something so simple, something I can't remember saying, or even something I can't imagine myself saying. The Lord has his way of using our words to bear his message of love. Yes, we have been baptized into Christ, and we can be Christ to one another.

What's the latest? I opened my Bible this morning and God said . . .

39 | *Come and Eat*

JOHN 21:1–14

*After these things Jesus showed himself again to the
disciples by the Sea of Tiberias; and he showed himself in this way. Gathered there together were Simon
Peter, Thomas called the Twin, Nathanael of Cana
in Galilee, the sons of Zebedee, and two others of
his disciples. Simon Peter said to them, "I am going
fishing." They said to him, "We will go with you."
They went out and got into the boat, but that night
they caught nothing.*

*Just after daybreak, Jesus stood on the beach;
but the disciples did not know that it was Jesus.
Jesus said to them, "Children, you have no fish, have
you?" They answered him, "No." He said to them,
"Cast the net to the right side of the boat, and you
will find some." So they cast it, and now they were
not able to haul it in because there were so many
fish. That disciple whom Jesus loved said to Peter,
"It is the Lord!" When Simon Peter heard that it was
the Lord, he put on some clothes, for he was naked,
and jumped into the sea. But the other disciples came
in the boat, dragging the net full of fish, for they
were not far from the land, only about a hundred
yards off.*

*When they had gone ashore, they saw a charcoal
fire there, with fish on it, and bread. Jesus said to
them, "Bring some of the fish that you have just
caught." So Simon Peter went aboard and hauled the
net ashore, full of large fish, a hundred fifty-three of*

them; and though there were so many, the net was not torn.
Jesus said to them, "Come and have breakfast." Now none
of the disciples dared to ask him, "Who are you?" because
they knew it was the Lord. Jesus came and took the bread
and gave it to them, and did the same with the fish. This was
now the third time that Jesus appeared to the disciples after
he was raised from the dead.

Jesus had sent a message to the apostles that they were
to go to Galilee and wait for him there. That made
sense. Capernaum had become very much his home base,
and it was hometown for a number of them. So off to
Galilee they went. And waited. And got tired of waiting.
Especially the ever up-and-at-'em Peter. "I am going fishing," he announced, and immediately they were all with
him, out into the boat and out to sea.

It was one of those nights, though, when the fish
seemed to have gone on holiday. Not a one came into
their nets. At dawn's early light a rather discouraged
crew looked toward the shore. It was time to go home—
empty-handed. It didn't exactly help morale when a lone
stranger (it was early and they had rather hoped to make
it in without being seen) shouted across the waters: "You
didn't catch any fish, did you?"

A possible customer he might have been, but they
were not interested in customers right then. An unambig-
uous "No" was their reply. And then came the strange
advice: "Cast your net on the other side."

Was there, deep down in them, some vague echo of
another day when they had heard similar advice? Or was
it simply that a dejected crew was ready to give it one
more try?

Soon the net was not just holding; it was almost
pulling the boat down. What a catch! It did not take

long then to put two and two together. The "disciple whom Jesus loved"—and who loved him—knew: "It is the Lord!"

Again Peter was up-and-at-'em. He couldn't wait for the boat to pull in its great catch. He was already in the water and making for the shore.

And what did they find there? A charcoal fire and fish and bread slowly baking. Breakfast was on! This was the risen Lord, the one who had proved all his divine assertions without doubt, the Lord and Master. And yet he had gathered sticks, kindled a fire, and somehow found some fish and bread dough. He was fixing breakfast for his friends. Indeed, he himself served it, to each.

Things had not essentially changed. The divine was still a beggar for friendship. And, yes, there was that wonderful delicate touch: "Bring some of the fish that you have just caught."

Jesus has risen. He has ascended. He sits at the right hand of the Father. He is the glorified Lord of heaven and earth. And yet he is still with us, until the end of time. He promised. He is here as a friend, a serving friend. And— what I find more wonderful—he wants us to participate, bringing the gifts he has given us, in serving his friends. It is a wonderful community of mutuality, his circle. A most caring Lord invites us all to join in the care.

Come and eat! Jesus still says it: Come and eat me, come and eat the Eucharist, come and eat my word. But he doesn't stop there. He says it to all the poor and needy; indeed, he says it to all of us as he gives us our daily bread. He endows us with all the goods of his creating. And he invites each of us to contribute to the feast, bringing some of the abundance we have been able to gather with his help to help him feed his friends, especially those most in need.

A Christian is certainly one who follows Christ, accepts him as risen Lord and Master. And Christianity is built on friendship: Jesus calls us his friends. The Lord wants to share with us in a very human as well as divine way. An important part of that human sharing is our bringing to the gathering of friends a portion of what he has enabled us to have.

Come and eat! May the warmth, the caring, the tenderness of that day never be absent from our gathering about our risen Lord, who is ever in our midst.

40 | *A Moment That Changed My Life*

GALATIANS 2:19–21

For through the law I died to the law, so that I might live to God. I have been crucified with Christ; and it is no longer I who live, but it is Christ who lives in me. And the life I now live in the flesh I live by faith in the Son of God, who loved me and gave himself for me. I do not nullify the grace of God; for if justification comes through the law, then Christ died for nothing.

It really amazes me how a moment's insight can change a lifetime's patterns—its values, its way of seeing and acting. But that happens, especially when it is a moment seized by God's grace.

The other day I sat down in the solarium to drink a cup of orange juice while reading a bit of Dick Hauser's *In His Spirit*. It was as if this friend had sat down with me that morning to help me hear the Spirit through the texts of Scripture that had spoken to him. That is what it is like when we use a text other than the Bible for *lectio:* having a conversation with a friend.

My friend pointed out to me that, as a Christian, my understanding of who I am, my true self, is radically different from that of others.

It should be. I have been baptized into Christ, "and it is no longer I who live, but it is Christ who lives in me."

As Dick's words and the words of the Scripture that he had chosen spoke to me, I came to a whole new, deeply exciting realization of who I am. I am alive in the Trinity, in the embrace of Father and Son, Source and Begotten, total love given and received.

In practice, I had in many ways bought into the sense of self that is prevalent in our world today. I felt I had to prove myself by doing things. I was the prime mover in my activities. Sure, the grace of God was there somewhere. I knew I could not do anything apart from Christ. And what I did, I did for God. But I was the one who did it.

But this isn't the reality!

Holy Spirit has been given to us. By Holy Spirit we cry: *Abba*—Father. And everything else we do as Christian persons we do by Holy Spirit. There has been, to use William of St. Thierry's favorite phrase, a unity of spirit. In the likeness of the Three who are One, Christ and I have become one, even while we remain two. This is what he prayed for at the Last Supper: "The glory that you have given me I have given them, so that they may be one, as we are one, I in them and you in me, that they may become completely one, so that the world may know that you have sent me and have loved them even as you have loved me" (John 17:22–23).

God is not someone out there, up there, some other place. God is within. And not just as a delightful guest or resident. No! God and I have in some way really become one. I live now, not I, but Christ-God lives within me, and his Spirit is now my spirit.

I don't pretend to understand all this. It is really beyond my comprehension. But it is a reality. It gives me a whole new sense of my goodness. It gives me a new way in which I can trust myself, trust the instinct from within that guides me. It is an instinct for the good, for love, for life.

I am sure this knowledge has been here all along, quietly growing and becoming more effective in my life as a Christian, a Christ-person. I am sure I have heard or read these ideas and concepts before, expressed in one way or another. But as I drank my orange juice that morning, they emerged into consciousness in a way they had never done before.

Of course, this is something of the grace of *lectio:* what we have known all along, we suddenly *know.* And in a moment, our lives are changed.

ABOUT PARACLETE PRESS

WHO WE ARE

As the publishing arm of the Community of Jesus, Paraclete Press presents a full expression of Christian belief and practice—from Catholic to Evangelical, from Protestant to Orthodox, reflecting the ecumenical charism of the Community and its dedication to sacred music, the fine arts, and the written word. We publish books, recordings, sheet music, and video/DVDs that nourish the vibrant life of the church and its people.

WHAT WE ARE DOING

Books | PARACLETE PRESS BOOKS show the richness and depth of what it means to be Christian. While Benedictine spirituality is at the heart of who we are and all that we do, our books reflect the Christian experience across many cultures, time periods, and houses of worship.

We have many series, including *Paraclete Essentials*; *Paraclete Fiction*; *Paraclete Poetry*; *Paraclete Giants*; and for children and adults, *All God's Creatures*, books about animals and faith; and *San Damiano Books*, focusing on Franciscan spirituality. Others include *Voices from the Monastery* (men and women monastics writing about living a spiritual life today), *Active Prayer*, and new for young readers: *The Pope's Cat*. We also specialize in gift books for children on the occasions of Baptism and First Communion, as well as other important times in a child's life, and books that bring creativity and liveliness to any adult spiritual life.

The MOUNT TABOR BOOKS series focuses on the arts and literature as well as liturgical worship and spirituality; it was created in conjunction with the Mount Tabor Ecumenical Centre for Art and Spirituality in Barga, Italy.

Music | The PARACLETE RECORDINGS label represents the internationally acclaimed choir *Gloriæ Dei Cantores*, the *Gloriæ Dei Cantores Schola*, and the other instrumental artists of the *Arts Empowering Life Foundation*.

Paraclete Press is the exclusive North American distributor for the Gregorian chant recordings from St. Peter's Abbey in Solesmes, France. Paraclete also carries all of the Solesmes chant publications for Mass and the Divine Office, as well as their academic research publications.

In addition, PARACLETE PRESS SHEET MUSIC publishes the work of today's finest composers of sacred choral music, annually reviewing over 1,000 works and releasing between 40 and 60 works for both choir and organ.

Video | Our video/DVDs offer spiritual help, healing, and biblical guidance for a broad range of life issues including grief and loss, marriage, forgiveness, facing death, understanding suicide, bullying, addictions, Alzheimer's, and Christian formation.

Learn more about us at our website:
www.paracletepress.com, or call us
toll-free at 1-800-451-5006.

SCAN
TO
READ
MORE

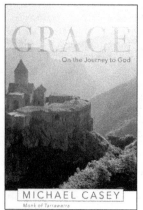

GRACE
ON THE JOURNEY TO GOD

Michael Casey, OCSO

ISBN 978-1-64060-064-5 | $16.99

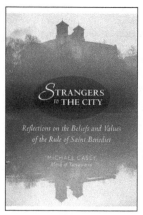

STRANGERS TO THE CITY
REFLECTIONS ON THE BELIEFS AND VALUES OF THE RULE OF SAINT BENEDICT

Michael Casey, OCSO

ISBN 978-1-61261-397-0 | $16.99

Available at bookstores
Paraclete Press | 1-800-451-5006
www.paracletepress.com

CPSIA information can be obtained
at www.ICGtesting.com
Printed in the USA
BVHW072209040521
606419BV00002B/420